Race, Wrongs, and Remedies

||||||||||||||||||||||||||||||||||||||||||||||||||||||||||

**HOOVER STUDIES
IN POLITICS, ECONOMICS,
AND SOCIETY**

General Editors
Peter Berkowitz and Tod Lindberg

HOOVER
INSTITUTION

OTHER TITLES IN THE SERIES

Race, Wrongs, and Remedies

Group Justice in the 21st Century

Amy L. Wax

HOOVER STUDIES IN POLITICS, ECONOMICS, AND SOCIETY

Published in cooperation with HOOVER INSTITUTION,
Stanford University · Stanford, California

ROWMAN & LITTLEFIELD PUBLISHERS, INC.
Lanham · Boulder · New York · Toronto · Plymouth, UK

ROWMAN & LITTLEFIELD PUBLISHERS, INC.

THE HOOVER INSTITUTION ON WAR, REVOLUTION AND PEACE, founded at Stanford University
in 1919 by Herbert Hoover, who went on to become the thirty-first president of the United States,
is an interdisciplinary research center for advanced study on domestic and international affairs. The
views expressed in its publications are entirely those of the authors and do not necessarily reflect the
views of the staff, officers, or Board of Overseers of the Hoover Institution.

www.hoover.org

Published in the United States of America by Rowman & Littlefield Publishers, Inc.
A wholly owned subsidiary of The Rowman & Littlefield Publishing Group, Inc.
4501 Forbes Boulevard, Suite 200, Lanham, Maryland 20706
www.rowmanlittlefield.com
Estover Road
Plymouth PL6 7PY
United Kingdom
Distributed by National Book Network

Copyright © 2009 by the Board of Trustees of the Leland Stanford Junior University

Published in cooperation with the Hoover Institution at Stanford University.

First printing, 2009
16 15 14 13 12 11 10 09   9 8 7 6 5 4 3 2 1
Manufactured in the United States of America

British Library Cataloguing in Publication Information Available

Library of Congress Cataloging-in-Publication Data Available

ISBN-13: 978-0-7425-6286-8 (cloth : alk. paper)
ISBN-10: 0-7425-6286-7 (cloth : alk. paper)

♾ ™ The paper used in this publication meets the minimum requirements of
American National Standard for Information Sciences—Permanence of Paper
for Printed Library Materials, ANSI / NISO Z39.48-1992.

CONTENTS

In his 1971 book *Blaming the Victim,* sociologist William Ryan defined blaming the victim as any attempt to "justify inequality by finding defects in the victims of inequality." Those who blame the victim, said Ryan, seek to "change [the victim's] attitudes, alter his values, fill up his cultural deficits, energize his apathetic soul, cure his character defects, train him and polish him and woo him from his . . . ways." It is characteristic of victim-blaming that "[p]rescriptions for cure are invariably conceived to revamp and revise the victim, never to change the surrounding circumstances."[1]

Ryan deplored blaming the victim. Attributing social inequalities to the actions of the victims themselves, he said, deflects attention away from the true causes and cures for poverty, inequality, and discrimination. These necessarily stand apart from the victim or his acts. Responsibility for the victim's injuries and for abating those injuries must be unequivocally charged to the real culprits: not the victims of injustice but those who have committed wrongs against them. Making the victim responsible for his state of disadvantage absolves the actual perpetrators.

Ryan opened his discussion with the example of lead poisoning in children. It is a mistake to fault mothers in the inner city for letting their children eat paint contaminated with lead. Rather, the focus should be on those who put lead in the paint and on those who use that paint in inner-city dwellings. Those agents should be held responsible. Although Ryan did not pursue this example in detail, he made clear that the proper placement of responsibility points the way toward solving the problem of lead poisoning. Effective steps to eliminate lead paint will take mother and child out of harm's way. Manufacturing and selling the dangerous product should be banned, and companies should be penalized if they violate those laws. Programs should be established to remove lead paint and replace it with a less harmful product. Those legal, regulatory, and programmatic measures are a complete solution to the problem.

Ryan was not the first to criticize blaming the victim. His book elaborated ideas that were already gaining wide currency. Those ideas continue in force. Victim-blaming has acquired such a bad name that the accusation is now tantamount in some circles to putting an argument completely off-limits. The victim-blaming epithet is a conversation stopper. If an approach blames the victim, it is by definition misguided, misleading, ahistorical, immoral, and unjust.

The proscription against victim-blaming has profoundly influenced thinking about the problem of racial disadvantage. The state of the black community continues to command widespread attention in America today. More than 150 years after the end of slavery and a generation after the civil rights movement, some blacks have improved their position, but others have lost ground. As a group, blacks continue to lag behind on many measures of social and economic well-being. Black men are disproportionately uneducated, unmarried, unemployed, and incarcerated.[2] Black women and children have high rates of poverty, and fatherless families abound. Views on what should be done about these conditions are stated and restated in the media, on talk shows, in popular and academic articles, and in an endless stream of opinion pieces and letters to the editor. Although everyone shares the goal of racial equality, there is stark disagreement on how to achieve this. The dominant view is that race disparities can be eliminated only through far-ranging efforts by government, private organizations, and society as a whole. Society must eradicate racism and provide effective, well-funded social programs to assist and improve the lot of the black community.

Voices dissenting from the dominant view insist that the key lies in behavioral reform and self-help. What is needed is a radical change in conduct, habits, and outlook. In that vein, Bill Cosby created a stir by denigrating the behavior of some members of the black community and implying that they are responsible for their own lack of success.[3] Those widely publicized remarks reignited the old debate, with commentators lining up on both sides.[4] New books by the journalist Juan Williams, and by Bill Cosby with co-author Alvin Pouissant, have continued the call for a fresh focus on black cultural renewal, internal reform, and self-help.[5]

This book represents a contribution to this debate. It argues that the taboo against blaming the victim has profoundly distorted thinking about race. Using core concepts from the law of remedies and drawing on a large body of social science evidence, it seeks to create a new paradigm for reconsidering the causes and cures of black disadvantage. Breaking the stalemate on how best to respond to persistent racial disparities requires dispelling the confusion surrounding blacks' own role in achieving racial equality. The key is to maintain a critical distinction between acknowledging society's responsibility for harms inflicted on black Americans, on the one hand, and appreciating blacks' unique power to undo that harm, on the other. Contrary to popular misconception, understanding that racial inequality is the product of society's past crimes is fully consistent with embracing self-betterment as the best strategy for tackling remaining disparities.

The analysis begins with the law of remedies. Legal doctrine recognizes a difference between causes and cures. That distinction finds expression in the sharp divide between liability, or responsibility for inflicting harm, and remedy, which encompasses undoing that harm. A fundamental tenet of the law of remedies is that a wrongdoer—someone who causes harm—is charged with the obligation to repair any injury he has caused. That standard defines the remedial ideal. But the law also recognizes that, for some injuries, the reality falls short of the ideal. The wrongdoer may be powerless to discharge that obligation. In some of those cases, the nature of the harms suffered is such that only the victim can repair them. Only the victim can cure himself.

This point, which is often overlooked in discussions of racial justice, applies to the present dilemma of black disadvantage. Much progress has been made in addressing racial inequality. But significant disparities remain. Because so many formal barriers have been eliminated, the problems that currently afflict the black community are different in type from those that prevailed in the past. Although those problems can be traced to historical mistreatment, effective cures will not come from the government, from white society, or from outsiders. Injury and remedy have diverged. Virtually all that ails black America today lies outside the power of others to fix. The key solutions rest with the victims themselves.

This conclusion follows from a rethinking of well-recognized facts. Social science evidence shows that enduring injuries to human capital now represent the most destructive legacy of racism. Although discrimination still exists, its role in perpetuating black disadvantage is now minimal as compared with factors that lie within the control of blacks themselves. Behaviors such as low educational attainment, poor socialization and work habits, criminality, paternal abandonment, family disarray, and nonmarital childbearing now loom larger than overt exclusion as barriers to racial equality.

As a historical matter, these patterns may well be rooted in slavery and social bias. But centuries of oppression and discrimination have worked their harm by distorting outlook, behavior, and values. Bad habits take on a life of their own, impeding the readiness to grasp widening opportunities as society progresses, discrimination abates, and old obstacles fall away. By holding people back and undermining their ability to compete, patterns of conduct and thinking now have a far greater role in perpetuating inequality than the racism and bias that dominated in the past.

Fruitful application of these insights requires facing up to the fact that society's power to address existing patterns, whether through publicly funded initiatives or otherwise, is severely limited. This means that the victims of discrimination are beyond the reach of outside help alone. Short of outright coercion, it is literally impossible for the government or outsiders to change dysfunctional behavior or make good decisions for individuals. These choices belong to persons, families, and the community itself. Because the present reality stands in marked contrast to the past, a radical shift in strategy is now in order. For the black community, a decisive inward turn is the program of choice, and self-correction is the only surefire tactic. Given the nature of the problem, the future belongs to self-help.

This conclusion meets understandable resistance. Are not the present troubles of black America the product of slavery and discrimination, imposed by white society? If the answer is yes—as it is generally understood to be—then the logic of remedial justice requires that society make amends. Because these practices inflicted grievous injuries on an entire people, stressing self-correction necessarily "lets society off the hook." Since others are responsible for what is wrong, touting self-help works a grave injustice. This objection underlies the outcry against Bill Cosby's remarks and the abhorrence of "victim-blaming." In light of the history of black oppression, implicating the victim in his own recovery is viewed as simple-minded and offensive.

The victim-blaming accusation, although understandable, is based on faulty logic. It reflects a failure to distinguish between liability and remedy or to appreciate the difference between identifying historical roots of problems and devising solutions to them. Specifically, that an individual may be entirely blameless for causing his own injury does not preclude placing much, most, or all of the responsibility on him for fixing his own problems or undoing the harms he has suffered. Indeed, there are situations in which assigning responsibility for repair to the victim is the only viable alternative: the nature of the injury is such that the wrongdoer is simply incapable of undoing that injury completely. Only the victim can cure himself.

As applied to the problem of racial disadvantage, the central insight is this: That blacks did not, in an important sense, cause their current predicament does not preclude charging them with alleviating it if nothing else will work. Accepting this does not deny the insults of the past. Nor does it mean that discrimination has entirely disappeared or that blacks as a group start out with equal advantages. Rather, the problems that readily yield to outside intervention have faded in importance, while those that require self-correction now dominate. Future racial progress calls for a decisive re-orientation in thinking and strategy. Only a concerted focus on self-help will close remaining gaps between blacks and other groups.

CHAPTER 1

The Remedial Ideal and the Demand for Racial Justice

Liability, Remedy, and the Rightful Position

American blacks are the victims of centuries of slavery and discriminatory treatment by private individuals and government. Although some question whether this mistreatment is the cause of the social problems blacks face today,[1] the overwhelming consensus is that current racial inequalities are the result of historical oppression. The questions addressed here concern the consequences of this understanding. What remedies follow from identifying the sources of racial injustice and from a description of racial wrongs? Doctrines central to remedial principles shed useful light on the problem. The proper analysis of these questions rests on a distinction between liability and remedy that is often overlooked in discussions of racial justice.

The law of remedies determines the obligations of legal actors who harm others in violation of the law's commands. Remedial doctrines seek not only to deter wrongful behavior but also to achieve justice by giving the victim his due. In pursuit of these objectives, two closely related concepts inform the law. The first is that the central goal of remedies is to return the victim to his rightful position. Relief should be structured to put the victim in the place he would have occupied if the harm had never been inflicted. Anything less falls short of the core remedial objective. Relief that does not "make the victim whole" is, then, less than ideal.[2]

The second key element of remedies doctrine is that the wrongdoer—the person or entity who inflicted the injury and caused the harm—must serve as the agent of remediation. The perpetrator must take steps to make the victim whole and restore him to his rightful position. In effect, he is charged with achieving the victim's complete recovery. His failure to undo all the harm he has inflicted falls short of the remedial ideal.

The make-whole ideal animates both equitable and legal doctrines. Under traditional principles of law, the wrongdoer must pay monetary damages to the victim in the amount that will compensate him completely for any harms inflicted. If money damages cannot make the victim whole, courts are authorized under the doctrine of equity to order injunctive relief—that is, courts have the power to command the wrongdoer to engage in or refrain from actions for the benefit of the victim. The appropriate scope of the make-whole remedy requires the construction of a hypothetical counterfactual scenario—a potentially vexed and controversial exercise.[3] But the general principle that guides this exercise is widely accepted. The objective is to restore the victim to the position he would have occupied if the wrong had never occurred.

Both equitable and legal doctrines recognize that the remedial ideal cannot always be realized. Remedial reality may fall short of the ideal. Remedies law is replete with cases in which wrongdoers cannot fully reverse harms to victims. It may not be obvious how to undo the damage or it may be literally impossible to repair the harm completely. A culprit's efforts may be doomed to futility because repair is beyond his power. A common example is that of physical injury. A severed arm cannot be reattached. A smashed eye cannot be reconstructed nor sight restored. A dead child cannot be brought back to life. In other cases, time or intervening events stand in the way of restoring the victim to his uninjured state. An item promised by contract may be lost or destroyed. A firm pledged to perform services may go out of business. In such instances, there may be no hope of fully rectifying or reversing the harms. The perpetrator cannot repair his wrong because he is literally powerless to restore the victim to his rightful position. He has created damage that he simply cannot undo. Recourse to "second best" remedies, including monetary compensation in lieu of full restoration, abound. That complete repair is not always achievable imparts a strong flavor of the tragic to the law of remedies.

One category of cases that falls short of the remedial ideal is the focus of this analysis: those in which the power to reverse the harm belongs not to the wrongdoer alone but in significant measure to the victim himself. In these cases, the wrongdoer may be able to compensate to some degree, but never completely. Only the victim can fully return himself to the rightful position. Repair cannot occur without the victim's active effort. In effect, the victim serves as gatekeeper to his own recovery. The wrongdoer must do his part— he must do whatever is necessary to enable the victim, through his own efforts, to make himself whole. But at some point, the victim's input becomes the rate-limiting step. There is nothing more the wrongdoer can do to speed the road back to full recovery.

One type of case in which the wrongdoer cannot effect a complete recovery and victims must participate in making themselves whole arises where an injury or its remediation involves the victim's thoughts, capacities, decisions, or actions. In such cases, the inflicted harm sometimes makes itself felt by compromising the development of human capacities (or human capital) or by distorting patterns of thinking and behavior. The next section provides an example of this category.

The Parable of the Pedestrian

As an example of a human capital injury, consider the following: As P crosses a street, D drives headlong through a red light and strikes him. D, who is unscathed, is entirely at fault in the accident. Unfortunately, the accident causes trauma to P's lower spine, leaving him unable to walk. He is rushed to the hospital and undergoes surgery. The surgery does little to alleviate his condition. He is then sent to a rehabilitation center. Upon arrival, P is told that he will never walk again unless he undergoes a protracted, tedious, exhausting, and painful course of physical rehabilitation, dieting, and exercise.

P's story involves a commonplace scenario drawn from the law of torts. Because D, the tortfeasor, is responsible and has engaged in wrongful action, he must compensate P for the expenses P incurred in the wake of his injury. D must pay P enough money to cover P's medical bills, his lost income, and the cost of his stay at the rehabilitation center.

Nonetheless, this recompense does not undo the harm. Nothing D can do or can be required to do will guarantee P's full recovery. Rather, full restoration requires P's sustained and willing participation. P will not be made whole—and will not be returned to his rightful position—until he walks again. His ability to walk depends on his own efforts. Unless he takes affirmative steps to effect his full recovery, it will not occur.

Call this the parable of the pedestrian. This is an instance of straightforward physical harm. Nonetheless, the remedy falls short of the ideal. D's inability to provide the victim with complete relief violates the central remedial imperative that the wrongdoer must make the victim whole. The remedial ideal contemplates that the victim will passively receive the wrongdoer's aid, and that this aid will suffice to undo the harm. Having already suffered injury from D's wrongful actions, P should not be made to contribute to his own recovery. Yet the pedestrian must now bear much of the cost of full rectification.

To compound the unfairness, the very accident that physically injured P and deprived him of the ability to walk has also caused him to become depressed, despondent, angry, resentful, and defeatist about the prospect of recovery and about his future. He has fallen into a psychological slough of despond. The accident has sapped his will. Not only has it deprived him of the use of his legs, but it has also seriously compromised the means to recover use of his legs.

That P must actively participate in his own recovery adds to his psychological distress. Discouraged and outraged, P inveighs against the forces of fate and the injustice of it all. The accident was not his fault. He is entirely blameless. Why should he have to exert all this effort and engage in so much sacrifice? The pedestrian resists the conclusion that his recovery depends on his own efforts. He insists that it is up to D to make him walk again. That is what justice requires.

In keeping with his conviction that D must restore him to health, P insists that D has not done enough. D must do more and there must be more that D can do. P casts about for measures that D can take. What P needs is a better-trained therapist, a better-equipped, up-to-date, state-of-the-art rehabilitation center, and access to the newest medical treatments and techniques. No matter what the expense, D must provide these things. Then P will be cured.

P's therapist commiserates. It is indeed unfair. But no matter. The therapist points out that D has, in effect, done his part—he has done everything he possibly can to enable P to recover. He has paid for P's medical care and his stint in the rehab center. He has replaced P's lost earnings. He has provided P with all that he needs. The therapist assures P that, based on her experience, there is nothing more D can effectively do to speed P's return to full functioning. She tells P that the costly and elaborate "extras" that P demands from D will have no significant effect on P's recovery. Additional help from D cannot ensure or guarantee success because D cannot make P walk again. P's input is now the rate-limiting step and there will be no further progress without P's effortful participation. Whether P walks again is ultimately up to P. No one can step into his shoes and do it for him. Is he up to the task? Maybe or maybe not. Either P will overcome or he will fail. That is the stark *reductio*.

As the parable of the pedestrian illustrates, victim-initiated remediation is sometimes unavoidable. The victim has no choice but to play a role in his own recovery. If he fails to do that, he will never return to full functioning. But assigning a critical role to the victim in undoing his injury does not identify him as the cause of the harm in the first place. Nor does it entail exonerating the true perpetrator. In the parable, D is unquestionably at fault. And D must compensate to the extent he can. D must create the conditions that allow P to return himself to the uninjured state.

This parable also illustrates a situation where recovery implicates human behavior. The pedestrian's initial insult is purely physical, but the process of recovery depends on P's attitudes and efforts. Without the victim's willing and sustained participation, full recovery is impossible. But the parable also applies to cases where wrongful actions more directly undermine psychological well-being, attitudes, or outlook. Ill treatment can sometimes distort a victim's thinking and feelings, which in turn influence life decisions and choices. The effects can be negative and destructive. Poor choices, unwise behaviors, or underdevelopment of capacities, abilities, and skills can compound and entrench the original harm.

Human capital or behavioral injuries of this type are said to occur in a broad variety of contexts in which harms make themselves felt by altering human response. Examples include the traumatic effects observed in connection with physical injury, disaster, sustained childhood deprivation, parental mistreatment, and forms of physical and sexual abuse. Attempts to recover from such crippling traumas are a staple of therapeutic intervention and a preoccupation of clinical psychology.[4]

How are such victims made whole? The nature of human capital injuries has important consequences for remediation. Repairing these harms implicates the victim's attitudes, actions, volition, and will. The victim may have to alter his thinking or feelings or re-form his behavior. Undoing the harm thus unavoidably enlists the victim's active participation. Implicit in the therapeutic strategy for addressing traumatic injury, for example, is the understanding that the victim plays an indispensable role in his own healing. He can-not remain passive. Indeed, he must actively resist the temptation to rely on those who inflicted the injury and he must refrain from open-ended and ever more elaborate demands for rescue. He must not dwell on what others can do or what money can buy. He must recognize that his own efforts are the rate-limiting step and that the wrongdoer simply cannot do for him what he must do for himself. Yet the victim, swayed by the remedial ideal and gripped by impera-tives of justice, may fail of this challenge or angrily reject it. This failure can fatally undermine the recovery effort.

The most profound (and disturbing) question lurking in such cases is whether the injury or deprivation is severe enough to nullify the very capacity for recovery. Can the victim really restore himself to health or wholeness? Or is his future now effectively beyond his control? In this context—as in the parallel case of race—the ques-tion is highly contested. Nonetheless, the assumption implicit in therapeutic interventions for psychological trauma due to stress, de-privation, or injury is that, in most cases, recovery is possible. In fac-ing the issue of whether or not to take the steps necessary to make himself whole, the victim retains the capacity to exercise free choice and will.[5] Human agency may be deformed, but it is not negated.

Can these practices shed light on the type of human capital inju-ries that are now ascribed to wrongs committed against disfavored social groups? In particular, do the assumptions underlying the ther-apeutic practice in response to trauma map onto the discrimina-tion and past wrongs suffered by American blacks? Can they help provide insights into the current social circumstances of the group? The next chapter examines these issues.

CHAPTER 2

Group Disadvantage and the Case of Race

Remedial Idealism and Race

Human capital injuries are frequently seen in the wake of race-based discrimination. It is common for historically despised or oppressed castes to display patterns of behavior and belief that undermine their ability to function effectively within competitive modern societies.[1] Similarly, a strong consensus has developed that there is a causal link between society's past treatment of blacks and present shortfalls in blacks' well-being. Those effects linger today. More specifically, it is widely accepted within popular accounts and academic discourse that racial discrimination has undermined the psychological well-being and distorted the behavior of American blacks.[2] Blacks as a group continue to lag in educational and occupational achievement and are plagued by high rates of criminality, drug addiction, family fragmentation, and economic dependence. The black community demands relief from these conditions, and society and the government are charged with providing it. This task is complicated, however, by the contribution of human capital and behavioral deficits to observed patterns. These elements not only impede the remedial project but also foster confusion in thinking about how best to address the enduring legacies of slavery and discrimination.

Although many scholars and ordinary citizens believe that racial persecution is the "root cause" of current racial inequalities, this idea is not wholly uncontroversial. There is disagreement over whether present problems can be traced chiefly to past insults or whether racism actively continues and contributes to present conditions. Among those who emphasize past causes, some question the very idea of responsibility across generations for harms inflicted on social groups. Others claim that intervening actions have dissipated liability or that subsequent events have made meaningful recompense impossible.[3] This book does not undertake an exhaustive review of these issues. Although it concludes that present discrimination is not an important force holding blacks back,[4] it acknowledges the pervasiveness of past racial oppression, and it takes as a starting point the assumption that the problems that beset black Americans today are the outgrowth of a long history of discriminatory treatment and enslavement. It accepts that there is a causal link between slavery, Jim Crow, historical private and public bias against blacks, and current conditions—including observed behavioral patterns—that perpetuate racial disparities. If blacks marry less often, commit more crimes, and perform less well in school and on the job market, the roots can be found in their past mistreatment. The present shortfalls are, in an important sense, not therefore the "fault" of the victims themselves. Outside wrongdoers are the culprits, and blame should be squarely placed on them.

The central concern of the analysis here, however, is with repair: Assuming this basic causal account, how can racial inequality arising from past wrongs be rectified? The remedial framework sheds light on some possible answers. According to the remedial ideal, those who created the problem must solve it. The wrongdoers—the government and society as a whole—have a duty to make things right. But remedies doctrine and practice also teach that the reality may fall short of the ideal. It is entirely possible that, in some cases at least, the wrongdoer cannot wholly make amends. Society cannot return victims to their uninjured state.

In the racial realm, this possibility is often forgotten. The belief in a just world is tenacious,[5] and remedial idealism holds sway. The quest for racial justice fuels a relentless and compelling demand. Because outsiders, and not blacks themselves, are responsible for present racial inequalities, those outsiders must eliminate them. The remedial ideal requires it.

This imperative exerts a powerful influence. It creates a force field that clouds thinking, distorts analysis, and generates fallacies and misconceptions that pervade discourse on race. One precept that dominates the analysis is the moralistic fallacy, the notion that "ought" implies "can." Justice demands that society fix what's broken. It therefore follows that society can achieve that result. That conclusion stems from the obdurate faith that justice can be done. Whoever caused the harm can put things right. The wrongdoer can completely undo his wrong. This fallacy goes hand in hand with a compelling rescue fantasy: society, through the instruments of government, has the power to cure what ails the black community. Whoever enslaved the great-grandparents of black children can make those children learn, behave well, and succeed. If the black family is disintegrating, outsiders can restore its stability. If crime plagues the black community, changing the system can cause crime to abate. If no formula has yet been found, the search must go on. Some combination of programs and policies must be discovered and will do the trick.

The moralistic fallacy combines with the rescue fantasy to generate a relentless external focus for solving racial problems. If the causes of the present dilemma lie outside the victim, solutions must as well. Because victims can bear no responsibility, they can play no originating role. In this mindset, policies, programs, and systemic reform are critical, and outside help is both necessary and sufficient to the task. To the extent that victims participate, they do so only in response to what is done to them or for them. Self-initiated change as the chief strategy for curing disparities is rejected as a form of "victim-blaming." This view regards the centrality of self-help as fundamentally inconsistent with principles of justice.

Remedial Idealism and Three Views of Discrimination

As noted, there is widespread agreement that the present dilemmas of black disadvantage can be traced to past injuries, including slavery, racism, and discrimination. Beyond that, consensus breaks down on why racial gaps between blacks and other groups persist and what to do about them. Although accounts of how current disparities arose and are perpetuated differ in emphasis and detail, most views on how to address these inequities ultimately converge. Society—and the government as its agent—must solve the problem. This imperative and the misconceptions it generates show the relentless influence of remedial idealism.

In one view, race-based discrimination remains pervasive, and conventional racism is still the chief engine of continuing black disadvantage.[6] Although "racism" and "discrimination" are often loosely defined, the focus of these terms is on the core of conduct prohibited by law: exclusion or unfavorable treatment "because of" race. Those who point to present discrimination, although acknowledging legal change, stress inadequate enforcement of civil rights laws and the persistence of informal slights. Proponents of the "present discrimination" view rely on recent social cognition research, which they claim shows that, although old-fashioned animus or overt prejudice may be less common than in the past, discrimination now finds expression in unconscious bias or unthinking disparities in treatment.[7]

A more expansive view sees discrimination and racism as primarily embodied in broader structures that represent the continuing legacy of past disadvantage. The theory of structural racism insists that group disadvantage can result from the application of seemingly neutral rules to carry forward historic practices.[8] Old-fashioned discrimination, which knowingly or inadvertently targets blacks for ill treatment, may be on the decline, but social and economic patterns shaped by old biases stand in the way of achieving racial equality.[9] The tangible and structural legacies of historical practices include housing segregation, fragmented social and political networks, lack of wealth and education, and the inferiority of institutions, such as inner-city schools, that predominantly serve minorities.

Yet a third approach stresses dysfunctional behaviors and maladaptive group practices as the most important legacies of racism. Proponents of this position point to accumulating evidence that behavioral factors now loom larger than overt exclusion as barriers to racial equality. Social scientists have documented the relative prevalence among blacks of low educational attainment, poor socialization and work habits, the underdevelopment of useful skills and human capital, high crime rates, drug use, paternal abandonment, family disarray, and nonmarital childbearing. Many who focus on behavior acknowledge that these patterns can be self-perpetuating. Although society progresses, discrimination abates, and old obstacles fall away, bad habits and dysfunctional attitudes shaped by past ill treatment persist and take on a life of their own. The inability or unwillingness of blacks fully to grasp new opportunities and take advantage of changed societal attitudes hobbles progress toward racial equality.

These three accounts, emphasizing discrimination, structural barriers, and behavior, implicitly point to two distinct types of obstacles to equality. One category comprises hard-and-fast impediments, imposed from the outside, that are insurmountable through individual or group effort. These obstacles are intransigent. They can be viewed as "brick walls." Discriminatory hiring practices based on pure racial animus are the prime example.

The other category consists of conditions or deficits that make it harder for persons to succeed or get ahead. These obstacles can, in turn, be divided into two types. First, there are conditions that are imposed upon individuals from without. Especially salient examples are deprivations of upbringing and social life, such as broken families, neighborhood poverty, poorly educated parents, inadequate early education, and lack of connection to people of means and social influence. Second, there are factors, thought to be shaped by these deprivations, that exert their grip from within. These include habits, attitudes, patterns of thinking, and behavioral tendencies that may issue in self-defeating behaviors. These can impede the acquisition of skills and learning, the formation of stable families, and progress in society or the greater world of work. Poor conditions of upbringing and socialization—including poverty, the lack of good examples, and the paucity of reliable life partners—confront black individuals with a "hard struggle." Deficits in character, outlook, and skills—which in turn comprise human capital and influence social and personal functioning—have a similar effect. But "hard struggles" are fundamentally different from unyielding impediments or "brick walls" that may stand in the way of personal success. First, hard struggles are often a function of the immediate social and cultural environment. But that environment has a dual aspect. It is imposed on members of the group, but also imposed by them. The attitudes and choices of relatives and close associates create the cultural setting in which individuals operate. Second, these types of obstacles can be, and today often are, altered or overcome through individual and collective determination and effort.

Much of the confusion surrounding remedies for racial injustice originates in a failure to appreciate the distinction between brick walls and hard struggles. Categorizing impediments is a conceptually slippery business that depends on descriptive focus and vantage point. In particular, one tendency is to lump together all factors that can be regarded as external to particular individuals—from old-fashioned discrimination to developmental inputs—for purposes of remedial analysis. For children, for instance, inauspicious starting points such as inattentive parents, inadequate socialization, or lack of stimulation in early childhood are external. Children do not control their early life circumstances and are not charged with doing so. Because these endowments, like conventional racial discrimination, are in some sense external, unchosen, and imposed, the temptation is to assume that similar strategies can address them. Despite their common element of externality, however, conventional discrimination and developmental disadvantage are radically different. Addressing them calls for distinct approaches.

More broadly, much of the confusion surrounding the analysis of racial inequality proceeds from the fact that the adversities that plague the black community are a mix of factors imposed from without and perpetuated from within. Indeed, the category of structural discrimination is often used to designate a range of conditions that blend chosen and unchosen elements. Poor schools, for example, may reflect resource disparities but also heavily implicate the conduct and performance of those attending the schools. "Poor upbringing" is inflicted on innocent children but is strongly dependent on the habits and conduct of adults. The label of "structure" is thus prone to misuse. It implies that disembodied forces are the sources of disadvantage. Yet oft-cited phenomena such as "crime" and "family breakdown" are not fixed and wholly external. They are not entirely imposed from without. They are a function of behavior. These very behaviors are the focus of those who see individual conduct and group norms as the primary engines of disadvantage.

Recognizing a fundamental distinction between brick walls and hard struggles is critical to clear thinking about remedies for racial inequality. Traditional types of discrimination, such as outsiders' outright refusal to hire or associate with minorities or legal deprivation of basic civil rights, were a form of brick wall: they were fixed impediments that could not be overcome by individual effort and collective determination. It was not within the victim's power to circumvent those historical obstacles, which posed an absolute bar to entry and participation in multiple sectors of the economy, the educational system, the housing market, and the workplace. But hard struggles are fundamentally different in kind. In the wake of decades of racial oppression, many blacks face conditions that make it more difficult for individuals to grasp opportunity, function as constructive citizens, and improve their life chances. These legacies are, in turn, material, institutional, and behavioral—or, more often, a confusing welter of all three. Although these factors can make progress more difficult, they can be—and often are—overcome. The main challenges facing minorities today fall into the category of hard struggles rather than brick walls. Therefore, equating past and present barriers to equality is a fundamental category mistake.

However the chief sources of inequality are understood, the key question of interest is what to do about them. Remedial idealism shapes both the dominant theory of causes and the prevailing prescriptions for cures, fueling the persistent urge to frame racial inequality as amenable to external solutions rather than to self-initiated internal or behavioral reform. This tendency is compatible with accounts that assign a principal role to discrimination, structure, culture, or all of the above. Whatever the precise diagnosis, the remedial formula points inexorably to the cure: massive external and material interventions—what can be done to and for people—rather than what they must do for themselves.

This mindset also assumes a symmetrical relationship between causes and solutions. On this view, everything can be made right just by reversing course. If discrimination is the culprit, then eliminating it is the cure. If racism is to blame, purging racism will do the trick. This is the myth of reverse causation. In its purest form, the quest for symmetry fuels the practice of identifying present racism—perhaps in a more subtle or unconscious form—as the main cause of inequality. The claim is that racial exclusion continues unabated and is no less important than the residue of past wrongs in perpetuating racial disadvantage. Conventional race-based discriminatory treatment is the cardinal "brick wall" impediment to racial progress. It stands as a hard-and-fast obstacle to equality. Because discrimination seems amenable to a simple, external fix that does not rely on the victim's active and continuous participation, it is the preferred first-line explanation for racial gaps. Identifying and rooting out all forms of discrimination is then assigned the highest priority and is elevated to the chief strategy of choice. The preoccupation with present discrimination generates strenuous efforts to document and demonstrate its existence using techniques ranging from measures of split-second unconscious association,[10] to sophisticated econometric analysis,[11] to field audit testing programs in housing, employment, and other areas of social life.[12] Thus does remedial idealism fuel the relentless search for the ever more elusive traces of racial bias and discrimination.

An external focus and reverse-causal thinking also plague the approach to structural racism. The remedial framework favors attention to material and external conditions, which are most easily dealt with from the outside. In the structural thesis, past wrongs are the ultimate source of racial disparities in political power, wealth, housing, neighborhood safety and quality, family structure and function, educational outcomes, and schools. Negating the effects of those wrongs and bringing about racial equality must lie with correcting these conditions. Interventions designed to address defective "structures" are primarily targeted to the material, rather than the behavioral, aspects of these problems. Those who point to structural discrimination see measures to equalize, upgrade, and redistribute the most palpable resources, including wealth, housing, jobs, and good schools, as the only effective method for eliminating the full range of dysfunctions. Not only will achieving equality on those fronts require sweeping institutional reforms, but those reforms will also prove sufficient. This thinking assumes that remedial effects will unfold in a particular sequence. That is, eliminating the structural institutional disparities most immediately amenable to public policy fixes will eventually result in the disappearance of racial disparities in family structure, criminal activity, educational achievement, and health. In effect, the belief is that, if material and economic conditions are improved, behavioral change will follow. With an adequate application of will and resources, achieving full racial equality is within the power of society as a whole and government in particular.

Remedial idealism, with its external orientation, also shapes the prescriptions embraced by those who assign an important role to culture and who see personal choices as key obstacles to black advancement. The focus on behavior often accompanies claims about the development of a distinct underclass, or ghetto, culture— a culture that is thought by some to extend its influence even to middle-class blacks. Elements that are sometimes identified with black culture, and are thought to contribute to black disadvantage, include weak adherence to bourgeois marriage and its conventions, oppositional attitudes, poor work and study habits, laxity toward adherence to law, and a lack of entrepreneurship and orientation toward the future.[13] Although this cultural cluster is not confined to blacks, the patterns are thought to be particularly entrenched within black communities, especially among the poor.[14]

Assigning a primary role to group differences in culture and behavior, although fitting less easily within the framework of remedial idealism, is not inconsistent with its imperatives. Indeed, the pull of the remedial ideal haunts discussions of how culture and behavior help perpetuate racial disadvantage. It is widely accepted (and conceded here) that cultural practices entrenched in black—and especially lower-class black—communities are the outgrowth of past social oppression. But this understanding often skews in favor of external solutions for the problems of behavioral dysfunction. As already noted, there are two variations on this theme, corresponding to the "present discrimination" and "structural" approaches to racial disadvantage generally. On one, untoward behaviors are not just the legacy of past conditions but also the product of present realities. Observed behaviors are maintained and, in some sense, necessitated by biases imposed from without. Present ongoing discrimination perpetuates dysfunctional behavior. The remedial corollary buys into the myth of reverse causation and runs this sequence in reverse: if racism and discrimination were truly rooted out, then adverse behaviors would disappear and racial gaps in social outcomes would close. A more nuanced alternative acknowledges that discrimination has abated but sees present structures as the direct product of past discriminatory behavior. It is these structures that maintain the dysfunctional culture. The solution is then to reform the system by establishing programs to eradicate present legacies of historical wrongs, including disparities in wealth, housing, education, and social and political influence. Once again, the sequence is run in reverse: eliminating the present products of racism, by whatever means necessary, will result in cultural reform and improved performance all around. Once the vestiges are rooted out, behavioral dysfunction will disappear.

The influence of remedial idealism on analyses of race and culture is thus pervasive, with most commentators seeing external interventions as critical to cultural reform. In this approach, outside help is necessary to address the behavioral dysfunctions wrought by racism. Even if shortfalls in human capital are best understood as the self-perpetuating, internal vestiges of historical practices, those effects can be negated by external assistance delivered from without, whether in the form of government sponsored or privately funded schemes of social engineering. The imperatives of this framework push toward imposed rather than homegrown solutions. Priority is assigned to greater expenditures on schools, housing, health care, poor support, training, and job creation. In any case, the approach is programmatic, with a stress on grand interventions and the large-scale transfer of resources from outsiders to those needing help.

An example of this kind of thinking can be found in the work of William Julius Wilson. Wilson concedes that deviant habits and behaviors—the hallmarks of the "culture of poverty"—impede progress toward racial equality.[15] According to him, the story begins with the migration of blacks from the south to northern cities in the early part of the twentieth century. Although blacks continued to live segregated lives, they found new economic opportunity in the form of factory jobs and other unskilled work. In Wilson's account, two key developments at mid century fostered the rise of a ghetto culture: the departure of the black middle class from the inner city after the enactment of civil rights laws, and the disappearance of urban manufacturing jobs that unskilled blacks had previously performed. The paucity of jobs, Wilson says, deprived inner-city residents of any incentive to develop effective work skills and habits. Because unemployed men could no longer support a family, marriage rates declined and childbearing outside marriage increased. The lack of good jobs bred criminal activity, which accelerated middle class flight from the cities. The departure of upstanding citizens fueled the trend toward dysfunctional behaviors among those left behind.

Wilson acknowledges the reality and role of culture. But his formula for cultural reform is to run the injurious sequence in reverse. Offer good jobs and a good education to inner-city residents and behavioral improvements will quickly follow. Ghetto dwellers will recognize the need to change their ways to take advantage of the new opportunities. A steady income will enable men to marry and support their children. Families will stabilize, and crime will abate. The black middle class will be drawn back into the city. This will accelerate the return to more functional cultural norms for lower-class blacks.

The path to recovery Wilson traces exemplifies the myth of reverse causation. Having identified material and external causes for the emergence of a culture of poverty, he posits a material and external route to its extinction. His position is grounded in remedial symmetry: economic and legal change caused the problem, so measures of the same type can reverse it. The wrongdoers—persons other than the victims—are the agents of harm, so those others must also be the agents of healing. Because economic and social conditions are the "root causes" of behavioral dysfunction, government must act to set those conditions right. Wilson's story strenuously avoids "blaming the victim." It assigns black inner-city residents little primary responsibility either for causes or for cures. Ghetto dwellers are reactors, not actors. They are not prime movers in their own recovery but rather responders to outsiders' or governmental efforts. In this view, victims cannot fail. They can only be failed by others.

Wilson's account of the relationship between problem and solution requires accepting questionable assumptions. First, altering economic conditions will lead to an almost automatic set of positive behavioral responses. Second, once social norms unravel, they can be restored simply by negating the conditions that led to their demise. Wilson ignores the possibility that some norms follow a path of hysteresis: the route that leads to disadvantage may be very different from the trajectory out of that state. Thus, although the disappearance of good jobs may have helped undermine sound work habits in the inner city, providing new jobs of similar quality (assuming that can be done) does not ensure that residents will perform these jobs to satisfaction. And although poor schools may have contributed to the under-education of blacks, upgrading schools will not necessarily lead blacks to study, read, and learn. Wilson is reluctant to concede that dysfunctional cultural practices may resist correction through outside intervention. He refuses to admit that some patterns cannot be broken merely by presenting economic opportunities and improving material conditions.

Wilson's analysis is characteristic of approaches to racial disparity across the board. Although he assigns an important role to culture and behavior, these function merely as placeholders in the remedial script. His prescriptions bring fully into play the myth of reverse causation, the moralistic fallacy, and a powerful rescue fantasy. Emblematic is the insistence that, without first effecting a dramatic *external* transformation, no serious behavioral reform can be urged or expected: Because it is incumbent on society to induce, cajole, and incentivize individuals to abandon dysfunctional practices, it follows that society can do so. Not only are social programs necessary to bring about the desired results, but they are also sufficient. Regardless of the nature of the problems, outsiders can fix what's broken.

Remedial Idealism and Sociological Thinking

Remedial idealism, with its relentless external focus, fits best with a peculiar vision of human behavior and a characteristic approach to human motivation. As applied to the problem of racial justice, it typically indulges an oversimplified social-scientific model of the interplay between human action and social conditions. This view sees human decision making as the product of material, social, and circumstantial constraints. Moreover, it considers individuals as rational actors motivated largely by a personal cost-benefit calculus. An important corollary of this framework is that individuals are similar in their decision-making structure: All persons, regardless of class, subculture, or racial group, will take steps to maximize individual well-being and will respond to opportunities or hardships in expected ways. In the rational-actor model, ambient conditions both explain and dictate human action. External constraints, not individual attitudes, are what matter most. Because similar outside forces will generally elicit standard patterns of behavioral response, it follows that disparate circumstances, not individual beliefs or cultural outlook, are the ultimate cause of divergent results. Observed behaviors, however seemingly dysfunctional, are best regarded as rational—and in some sense unavoidable—reactions to hardship, deprivation, or discrimination inflicted by others.[16] This construct enshrines the rule of *post hoc ergo propter hoc* in human affairs. Everyone is doing the best he can under the circumstances. Either persons cannot do otherwise or we cannot reasonably expect them to.

All this constitutes a hallmark of what David Brooks calls "sociological explanation."[17] This mode of thought currently dominates academic and general discourse on inequality, effectively displacing a moral, character-based focus on individual virtue and initiative. In seeing human decisionmaking as passive and mechanistic, with human action ultimately the product of extrinsic causes and determining conditions, this view leaves little room for freedom and meaningful choice. The idea of surmounting social background or besting adverse circumstances through self-motivated change figures little, or not at all, in this framework.

In regarding human decision making as quantifiable and amenable to systematic explication, sociological explanation holds special appeal for social psychologists who seek to develop a systematic, "objective" understanding of human choice that aspires to the rigor of established fields. The quest for a systematic social science of human behavior, although not disregarding culture altogether, acknowledges its force selectively and minimizes its influence when expedient. Especially when studying race, social scientists resist seeing culture as a primary force behind group success or failure and avoid attributing bad outcomes to deficient customs or values. This stance is partly grounded in the amorphous nature of culture, which defies precise analysis and quantification. There is as yet no fully satisfying account of the relationship of culture to behavior and no comprehensive theory of how distinct values arise, why they persist, and how they can be changed. Specifically, the origins of dysfunctional cultural practices and values are poorly understood.[18] But resistance also stems from respect for political sensitivities and a reluctance to label the behavior of the disadvantaged as dysfunctional. If all behaviors are the expected outgrowth of ambient conditions, it makes no sense to judge some as inherently or functionally less desirable or to assess some ways of life as superior to others. All behaviors are equally rational in light of their circumstances. Citing social forces rather than cultural deficiencies avoids "the invidious comparisons, political sensitivities, and bruised feelings often engendered by cultural explanations of success and failure."[19] Thus, the deterministic explanations for social dysfunction that dominate modern academic sociology represent the combined influence of the quest for scientific validity and the demands of political correctness.[20]

Likewise, sociological thinking is hostile to the idea that individual character is a critical determinant of human conduct. Social psychologists have seized on a few well-publicized experiments suggesting that people differ little in their response to stress, adversity, or temptation. These observations have fostered the ascendancy of situationism—the view that variations in circumstance rather than cultivated individual attributes best account for observed behavior.[21] Yet the embrace of situationism has been controversial. There is considerable evidence that individual characteristics and dispositions do predict behavior. Researchers in disparate fields, including experimental economics and developmental psychology, have documented a variety of responses to similar circumstances and have identified stable dispositions and individual character traits that consistently influence conduct.[22]

In its antipathy toward the idea that cultural values are key determinants of behavioral difference and in its commitment to situationism as a central principle of human affairs, sociological thinking makes little room for ideas like good character or self-betterment. If external circumstances both explain and dictate human response, then relying on spontaneous self-correction is unjust and incoherent. In denying the very possibility of self-directed personal improvement or group cultural reform, this approach rejects internally motivated change as the best solution to racial inequality. Indeed, most social scientists regard exhortations to self-betterment as naive or incoherent and talk of "boot-strapping" as embarrassing. On this view, the idea of a change of heart or a "conversion experience" belongs to an outmoded discourse of virtue, character, and moral uplift that refuses to see human action as the exclusive product of historical antecedents and social context. In neglecting the larger forces that condition human behavior, the belief in spontaneous self-correction shows itself to be unsystematic, unscientific, unso-phisticated, and hopelessly misguided.

The sociological approach feeds into a belief in the necessity and efficacy of external solutions to social problems and perpetuates the rescue fantasy that group equality can be bought through poli-cies and programs. Above all, it refuses to recognize the centrality of self-help to solving the problem of racial disadvantage. Like the logic of remedial idealism, sociological thinking inexorably favors imposed over homegrown solutions. If observed behavior is the expected result of existing patterns, then material and social cir-cumstances are crucial to outcomes. Because human beings are the playthings of social forces, the power to manipulate and transform human conduct must lie with outsiders or society as a whole. Dys-functional choices represent a rational response to social conditions, so individuals cannot be expected to abandon existing practices un-til conditions improve. It follows that real change is impossible with-out outside help. It is incumbent on others to produce the necessary transformations.

In viewing behavioral patterns as the product of external forces, sociological thinking threatens to collapse into a vulgar determin-ism. By leaving little room for meaningful human agency, it appears to negate choice altogether. In the context of racial inequality, this approach dissolves the distinction between the insurmountable and the difficult—between brick walls and hard struggles. It leads to the conclusion that coping with unhelpful social beginnings and progressing without wealth or privilege are no different from over-coming rigid obstacles. This conclusion generates two corollaries: No improvement in blacks' condition is possible without external change, and external change is sufficient to produce that improve-ment and achieve racial equality.

The sociological model combines with remedial idealism, the myth of reverse causation, the moralistic fallacy, and the rescue fantasy to shape the language, assumptions, and recommendations of those concerned with racial justice. Although cultural practices and behavioral dysfunction are acknowledged by some to contribute to the problem, these elements are assigned a stylized role in the dynamic of cause, explanation, and repair. Even when personal conduct is factored in, primary responsibility for addressing disadvantage is ultimately placed on others. The sequence of repair is external first, behavioral second.[23] Approaches that emphasize self-correction as the core strategy for combating racial disadvantage are dismissed as apologias for the ultra-conservative right.[24]

The belief in programmatic solutions for group disparity, coupled with a vision of the disadvantaged as imprisoned by circumstance, is evident in a steady stream of studies that pours from academia, think tanks, and policy institutes. Although this literature is not exclusively concerned with race, the dilemma of minorities looms large and creates a force field of conceptual influence. Even for the poor in general, where there is no comparable history of persecution and remedial imperatives do not necessarily apply,[25] the taboo against "blaming the victim" has a strong hold. Initiatives directed at transforming values and behavior are rarely touted as a centerpiece of reform.

A characteristic analysis can be found in a recent book focusing on black men. The authors present extensive data showing that black men lag in education, employment, family formation, and obedience to law. Although mentioning the need for behavioral reforms, the analysis gives pride of place to a laundry list of policy proposals, including improving schools, upgrading and extending training programs, providing more and better-paying jobs, and reducing men's burden of child-support payments.[26] Similarly, a study investigating poor single mothers in the Philadelphia area acknowledges men's behavior—including infidelity, lack of work ethic, violence, and financial irresponsibility—as a major source of instability in poor women's relationships.[27] Yet the authors maintain that the solution lies in outside help, not self-directed behavioral reform. Policymakers must find a way "to make low-skilled men safer prospects for long-term relationships with women and children." Specifically, the government must provide "more access to stable, living-wage employment."[28] As with William Julius Wilson, the authors of this study assume that the habits that make these men such "crummy boyfriends" and inferior husband material will fade away if opportunities expand and conditions improve. If good jobs at good wages appear, bad behavior will disappear. That men's poor attitudes and inadequate performance are the main reasons they fail to obtain and succeed at such jobs is a possibility that does not warrant serious discussion.[29]

Breaking the Grip of Remedial Idealism

The search for external interventions, policy initiatives, and programmatic solutions has been the hallmark of approaches to racial inequality for decades. This emphasis is understandable in light of the assumptions that dominate the field. The argument here is that this strategy is not only futile but counterproductive. Although emphasizing law and policy may once have made sense, the time has come to assign priority to self-improvement through behavioral, cultural, and moral reform. This position draws strength from a growing body of social-scientific evidence that points ever more strongly to one conclusion: On a variety of fronts in which blacks continue to lag significantly behind other groups, behavioral choices and human capital deficits are now far more important than external, structural impediments in perpetuating racial inequality. But, as the preceding discussion reveals, this evidence alone tells us nothing about solutions. The idea that society can take effective steps to work basic changes in behavior or to make up for important human capital deficits dies hard. Yet these expectations are fundamentally misguided. Not only do they fly in the face of basic realities of human cultural and social life, but they are also increasingly strained in light of decades of failed programs and public expenditures. The deficits that are presently most significant cannot be alleviated through known policy initiatives imposed from without. Rather, they are best addressed by private measures undertaken within the group and by individuals.

This position entails a fundamental rejection of sociological thinking. The principal drawback of the sociological view is its failure to recognize individual freedom and distinct cultural values as the most powerful determinants of social success and failure. The rational-actor model of human motivation and decision making cannot easily accommodate the undeniable fact that, throughout history and worldwide, some people and groups clearly have accomplished more than others under similar hardships and constraints. The concept of culture helps explain why individuals and groups take on life's struggles with varying degrees of success.[30] Likewise, a belief in situationism, or the primacy of social circumstances as determinants of conduct, fails to recognize that individuals do in fact differ in their responses to life's challenges and that choices are in part a function of character—that is, of the values, ideals, attitudes, and moral precepts individuals embrace and their willingness faithfully to act on them. In addition, there is little room in the sociological construct for normative judgments of human conduct or for the possibility of group or individual dysfunction. Yet it is hard to deny that some cultural practices do interfere with personal development and perpetuate group disadvantage. Some patterns of thought and behavior are less conducive than others to human flourishing.

The remainder of this book draws on an extensive body of evidence now available, in conjunction with the conceptual framework set forth here, to argue that self-transformation must now be the strategy of choice for addressing racial inequality. Negating disadvantage is no longer a matter of surmounting social and political brick walls but rather of dealing with hard struggles that yield to changes in outlook, initiative, and effort. Building the case that reducing inequality lies largely within the victims' own control requires navigating a complex body of data on the present nature of racial inequality and the effectiveness of public policy measures designed to address it. As already noted, there are striking average differences between blacks and other groups in family structure, educational attainment and achievement, criminal activity, and work patterns. For a range of indicators pertinent to social and economic well-being, ongoing discrimination—whether overt or unconscious, deliberate or inadvertent—explains very little of these present inequalities. Rather, numerous studies show that opportunities for racial minorities have dramatically expanded and that conventional barriers to advancement—in the form of overt exclusion and discrimination in jobs, housing, and education—have abated substantially since the 1960s. These "brick walls" now account for an insignificant portion of disparities by race in important areas of social life.[31] A consensus has developed that what little discrimination remains most often takes the form "rational" or "statistical" discrimination—that is, social decision making that uses race as a predictor of behavior or a proxy for productivity-related abilities. Yet the impact of this bias is still negligible as compared with deficits in human capital and soft skills that prevent blacks from competing effectively for existing opportunities. These deficits now loom larger than overt exclusion as the most important sources of continuing racial inequality.

In response to findings on the waning of conventional discrimination and the opening of new opportunities to blacks, the proponents of racial justice cling to well-worn arguments. Even if conventional forms of discrimination have abated, they say, blacks face important structural impediments as holdovers from past racism. They attend poorer schools, live in undesirable neighborhoods, possess fewer resources, and have less wealth and less advantageous social connections. Until these differences are eliminated, inequality will persist. This position often generates the contention that, under ordinary remedial principles, society must do more—far more—than simply provide equal opportunity by guaranteeing a fair process for advancement. If the goal is really to eliminate disadvantage in the fullest sense of the word, the argument goes, the mere opportunity for self-improvement is not good enough. Much more must be done to make up for present deficits. Just as the driver must create the most propitious conditions for the pedestrian's recovery, so also must society smooth the way towards the closing of racial gaps, even to the point of providing special advantages, privileges, or resources to members of the injured group.

The case for intervening to whatever extent necessary to remedy racial disparities in material or social conditions is compelling in the racial context. Justice dictates that change be made as easy as possible. That means that all palpable obstacles to behavioral improvement and all forms of unequal opportunity must be addressed and removed. The remedial ideal requires society to "level the playing field." It must find a way to make up for and negate all differences in starting points.

This demand is a formula for frustration and dashed hopes because, under current conditions, it is never-ending. The question is not whether others could offer more assistance or whether extra measures would *appear* to make things easier. Rather, it is whether the proposed help will *in fact* make a difference and produce a better outcome. Although the power to ease hard struggles would appear to rest with more privileged and better-endowed outsiders, additional efforts to improve conditions, however well-intentioned, ambitious, and expensive, routinely deliver far less than promised. That is because externals are not the rate-limiting step. As with the injured pedestrian, recovery will not occur unless the victim does his part. Absent that, the wrongdoer's help will make no real difference. Any further inputs, however elaborate and expensive, will yield rapidly diminishing returns and ultimately prove futile. Without a change in the victim's own attitudes and behaviors, there will be no progress.

We have reached such a juncture in the quest for racial justice. Given the nature of the current legacy from past racial harms, the effectiveness of outside intervention is now strictly limited. Further efforts, however strenuous, are sure to disappoint. Without a radical change in blacks' own approach to their continuing dilemma, the problem of racial inequality will continue to resist policy-based solutions.

The track record so far with programs to address chronic problems of underachievement, criminality, and family disarray bears this out. These conditions are increasingly unresponsive to any known policy interventions and persistently resist fixes imposed from without. Despite decades of programs, government has not discovered how to change entrenched patterns, make better choices for individuals, or induce people to grasp opportunities. Nor has it learned how to shape attitudes that bear on social success. Even well-thought-out, targeted programs informed by the latest social science research—such as intensive preschool education or dispersion of poor families into middle-class neighborhoods—have produced, at most, modest and transient results. In the area of behavioral reform, experience confirms sociologist Peter Ross's Iron Law of Evaluation: "The expected value of any net impact assessment of any large-scale social program is zero."[32]

That government programs cannot effect the necessary behavioral changes should come as no surprise. No one knows how to ensure that others make good choices or engage in constructive behavior. Nor do we know how to make someone obey the law, study hard, develop useful skills, be courteous, speak and write well, work steadily, marry and stay married, be a devoted husband and father, and refrain from bearing children he cannot or will not support. These behaviors originate in private decisions, which are in turn shaped by family upbringing, early childhood experiences, and the immediate social circle. Such informal influences are particularly crucial in establishing key habits and understandings. No known policy can transform these powerful inputs, and governmental efforts have repeatedly failed to override or negate them. To the extent that values and culture dominate in producing dysfunctional behavior, there is little evidence to date that the government can effectively intervene. Although society can create the conditions that enable persons to behave constructively if they choose, outsiders cannot bring those behaviors about.[33] There are some things people can only do for themselves.

This line of argument focuses on behavioral reforms. Implicit in this view is the understanding that racism has distorted patterns of belief and conduct and that these pattens must change before group equality can be achieved. But some who insist that society intervene to equalize racial outcomes adopt a radically different tack. They reject the idea that there is anything wrong with the victim and regard any efforts to alter their conduct as fundamentally misguided.

On this view, the problem lies in labelling behaviors as dysfunctional. The idea that some patterns of living are more desirable than others is "constructed": Society chooses to reward some choices or attributes and to stigmatize or devalue others. This rhetorical move is especially salient in discussions of the black family. According to this view, fatherless families are not inherently inferior to conventional two-parent families. Rather, they have the capacity to function just as well. To the extent that children of single mothers have worse outcomes, government could negate this result by compensating for any deficits. If single-parent families are poorer, government can give them more money. If their children suffer from less parental attention and supervision, the government can create programs to supply what's missing. Thus, even if government cannot transform behavior, it has the power to hold people harmless for whatever choices they make.[34] Likewise, in the educational context, government may not know how to raise student achievement. But, it is argued, society's decision to dole out rewards and opportunities based on objective measures of learning and academic performance is not preordained. Institutions could choose to ignore or downplay deficits in these areas in favor of other attributes, including race itself. To the extent that group differences in academic outcomes can be seen as the product of past mistreatment, institutions have the duty to give them less weight in allocating social rewards.

These arguments embody another form of rescue fantasy. Just

as government cannot produce more functional behavior, it likewise cannot equalize the consequences of all personal choices or hold people completely harmless for deficits in performance. Redefining merit to cast aspersions on the usual metrics cannot change the fact that people with more knowledge and skills on average perform better in a range of social roles widely valued by others. It is difficult, if not impossible, for the government to negate all effects that flow from these differentials without drastically transforming our democratic, capitalist society and exerting tyrannical control over all social outcomes. Likewise, as discussed below, the greater success of traditional nuclear families in developing human capital and securing their members' well-being is not the product of arbitrary conventions but rather is grounded in the inherently superior functioning of such families. These advantages do not flow from societal privilege or the stigma attached to other family forms, nor are they traceable chiefly to better material resources. Rather, the evidence suggests that the traditional two-parent family does the best job of nurturing children. No known policy instruments can make up for the lack of a marital bond, shared biological ties, long-term parental cooperation, or a consistently present, loving father. Social programs and government services cannot equalize the life chances of children growing up in less desirable situations. Such programs can never replace the real thing.

The erroneous view that programmatic interventions can substitute for spontaneous cultural and behavioral transformation is not subject to definitive refutation or disproof. The diehard faith in the power of external assistance can never, by its nature, be entirely dispelled. Showing that government or external private initiatives can do little to alleviate the plight of disadvantaged blacks requires proving a negative—that there is no conceivable policy that will work. Such a proposition is impossible to demonstrate and prompts the expected response: that programmatic remedies for racial injustice have not yet succeeded does not mean they never will. That nothing we have tried has worked does not mean we should stop trying.

Because everyone wants to believe that racial equality is achievable, hope springs eternal that the proper combination of will, commitment, insight, expertise, and resources can produce that result. We need only discover the right formula, and equality will prevail. This faith fosters the belief in reverse causation and an embrace of the attendant rescue fantasy. If the necessary external changes occur, internal transformations will follow. The government has the duty, and hence the ability, to hold people harmless for whatever patterns have emerged from past wrongs. Either the government can change untoward behaviors or it can and must fully compensate for them. These convictions fuel repeated calls for new initiatives to address structural inequalities.

The self-help position, in contrast, asserts that remaining disparities will yield only to straightforward changes in behavior. If individuals make different decisions and better choices, outcomes will improve and inequalities will steadily abate.[35] A new way of life is not only necessary but also largely sufficient. If blacks transform their cultural understandings, actions, and commitments, any remaining impediments to group parity will prove unimportant and can, as a practical matter, be overcome.

Some key assumptions underlie a commitment to self-help as the main strategy for achieving racial equality. First, this approach requires turning away from sociological thinking, with its stress on structural impediments and the determinism of social causation. The self-help position rests on the recognition that, although circumstances can and do influence life decisions, they do not negate choice. What is difficult is not impossible. There is a meaningful difference between brick walls and hard struggles. Under conditions prevailing in the United States today, people's circumstances need not rigidly dictate, control, or necessitate habits of living and thinking. No able-bodied person is doomed to failure. Patterns that undermine individual advancement and group progress are amenable to change. Individuals must come to believe that, through the exercise of reason and understanding, they can and should make different and better choices. Individual "conversion experiences" can occur. Self-initiated reform is a real possibility, and not just a theoretical idea.[36]

Second, the self-help approach requires that basic economic opportunities be available and that avenues for self-development be open to persons of all backgrounds who are determined to make a decent life and get ahead. At a minimum, society must provide a reasonably well-functioning economy that makes employment widely available to persons with divergent levels of skills. Within this scheme, the government has a role in pursuing policies of a general kind that ensure basic economic well-being. These arguably may include measures, such as subsidies for working families or progressive tax policies designed to "make work pay," that permit all employed persons to meet basic needs and to provide their children with the opportunity to attain economic self-sufficiency.[37]

In addition to ensuring that people who "play by the rules" can live minimally decent lives, society should also provide the prerequisites for self-development. It must maintain social institutions designed to prepare people for the world of work, including well-functioning public schools that give everyone the opportunity to develop the skills for constructive citizenship and to pursue economic advancement. The path to higher education should likewise be open to all those who have attained enough proficiency to complete advanced schooling.

The evidence shows that the prerequisites for self-help largely prevail in the United States today. Basic educational and employment opportunities are ordinarily widely available, and jobs of some kind can be obtained by virtually all who aggressively seek them. Although occasional recessionary periods (such as the recent economic crisis and slowdown) can make jobs harder to obtain, such episodes have not so far dominated our economy and have generally proved short-lived. Public schools provide basic instruction to those determined to learn, and few capable students are turned away from college due to inability to pay. In addition, there are tax and transfer policies in place, such as food stamps, housing subsidies, and the Earned Income Tax Credit, that ensure that those who behave prudently will enjoy a basic minimum standard of living.[38]

Although achieving a minimally decent life may sometimes require great effort, especially among the less skilled, the necessary steps are well within the reach of most ordinary persons regardless of background or origins. An oft-repeated formula for attaining this status involves three elements: Complete high school, take a job and hold it, and marry after graduating and before bearing children.[39] This formula acknowledges that personal conduct matters. Becoming a single parent, being voluntarily idle, dropping out of school, using and selling illegal drugs, and breaking the law all significantly compromise success. Today blacks tend to engage in these antisocial behaviors at higher rates than other major American groups. If avoiding these tendencies will not necessarily bring about racial equality, it will go a long way toward closing existing gaps. And it will set the stage for further improvement by enhancing the well-being of children and positioning more blacks to do well academically and to attend and graduate from college.[40]

Although following these simple rules for advancement would seem to be well within the grasp of all ordinary, able-bodied people, not everyone manages to meet the challenge. Some life circumstances can make it more difficult to comply with even these simple recommendations. Because blacks, on average, are significantly less likely than others to do so, the quest for racial equality fuels the impulse to identify any and all obstacles to these achievements and then to undertake initiatives to alleviate them. Thus, even among those willing to concede that these basic steps are advisable or even necessary, the argument for more assistance and more programs for blacks—or for the disadvantaged generally—continues. Indeed, it is hard to understand why we would resist doing more: Why not do all we can to make self-improvement easier?

Unfortunately, such initiatives are almost certain to disappoint. The grip of remedial idealism is powerful, and the tendency persists

to see the hard struggles facing blacks as purely a product of social forces and external obstacles and as capable of correction only
through improvements in those conditions. For example, blacks are
objectively less well off and materially poorer than others. There
would appear to be so much more the government could do to
make up for this, including contributing more resources, providing
a better education, and ensuring fresh opportunities. Yet, as with
the injured pedestrian, the promise of such initiatives is illusory.
The factors that make self-improvement difficult are a complex mix
of internal characteristics and present circumstances. These cannot
easily be disentangled and do not yield to straightforward manipulation. As created, imposed, and constrained by the myriad private
choices of family and community members, the impediments to
progress are closely intertwined with behaviors and critically dependent on them at every point. The rhetorical habit of identifying blacks as victims of poverty, poor neighborhoods, crime, failing schools, broken families, and other disembodied forces ignores
the truism that people largely make their own environment. These
commonly identified conditions are not solely or even predominantly imposed from above. Rather, they are mostly the product of
the actions and choices of participants.

The safety of neighborhoods and the quality of schools depend
on the conduct and outlook of the people within them. The structure of families and their success in safeguarding their members'
personal and financial well-being rest on how family members conduct themselves over time and generations. Economic security and
achievement are largely the result of individual entrepreneurship,
sustained work, group cooperation, prudence, and restraint. Thus,
many factors that are categorized as structural vary with individual
initiative and ultimately depend on self-help. Identifying these factors and manipulating them from the outside are difficult if not impossible tasks.

As with the parable of the pedestrian, the behavior of those
targeted for assistance, or of those in their immediate social circle,

effectively functions as the rate-limiting step. This means that pro-grammatic efforts to make the struggle easier are often futile or at best offer minimal returns. In any event, the quest to equalize all circumstances—to ease all hard struggles and to "level the play-ing field" in every respect—is by definition endless and elusive. Al-though society can take various steps to reduce hardships and in-crease opportunities, it cannot banish all inequalities or dispel all obstacles. Persons and groups are endowed with a complement of strengths and weaknesses, which they must parlay through the myriad choices that they make. Many deficits are self-imposed as well as conferred. Disadvantages are both self-generated and inher-ited. These influences work together and cannot readily be teased apart. The multiplication of bureaucracies and programs to deal with every conceivable adversity and to erase every deficit imposes ever-growing costs with ever-diminishing returns. This is precisely the wrong approach. In the United States today, what others can do to help disadvantaged groups achieve equality pales as compared with what they can do for themselves.

The strongest evidence that self-directed efforts can work on prevailing conditions is that available opportunities for self-advancement are routinely grasped by persons from humble back-grounds and with few practical and material advantages. Persons facing similar obstacles, armed with variable attitudes and outlooks, are observed to respond very differently to similar external con-straints. The difficulties blacks encounter are not radically different from those faced by others, including persons from other minority groups who have recently immigrated to the United States. Some of those newcomers do relatively better than black Americans on many socioeconomic indicators despite little education and few ac-cumulated resources. Even among those who begin without advan-tages or initially fail to grasp opportunities, self-defeating behavior is not irreversible. Over a lifetime, many individuals change course or achieve internal reform. Different outcomes among persons with similar starting points suggest that the basic prerequisites for self-improvement are already in place and that what matters most is how well people grasp opportunity. As Shelby Steele states, there is "no excuse any more for not doing well in this society."[41]

The next chapter marshals social science evidence from a variety of fields to support the argument that behavioral reform is now the key to achieving racial equality in economic and social outcomes. The data demonstrate that the chief remaining impediments to black equality are not the hard and fast obstacles that hobbled black progress until a few decades ago. Racial discrimination now accounts for very little of the gap between blacks and other groups. The most significant remaining discrepancies can be traced to measurable deficits in human capital and to patterns of social behavior that bear on performance and life success. These patterns are bound up with dispositions and choices that are shaped and constrained by private social influence. The dominant notion that the main forces now holding blacks back will yield to bold institutional change and massive outside assistance is misguided and conceptually muddled. Experience to date, and plain common sense, show that the key problems largely resist alleviation through available social policy instruments. In sum, closing existing racial gaps no longer depends on surmounting brick walls. This achievement requires hard struggles by the victims themselves. As with the parable of the pedestrian, the victims' contribution is now the rate-limiting step on the road to equality. Additional efforts from society or government are unlikely to yield further progress.

CHAPTER 3

Racial Disparities and Human Capital Deficits

Much of the last century saw steady improvement in blacks' educational achievement, earnings, and job status as reflected in the growth of the black middle class.[1] In the past few decades, that progress has slowed or leveled off, with significant gaps remaining and even widening on some measures. As a result, black Americans continue to lag behind other racial and ethnic groups in indicators of social and economic well-being. The focus of this chapter is on a few key areas of persistent inequality: education, employment, and family structure.

Deficits in Education

From the 1950s until the mid 1980s, blacks posted gradual but steady gains in both educational attainment (as reflected in years of schooling completed) and educational achievement (as measured by test scores) relative to whites nationwide.[2] In the past two decades, that trend has faltered, with progress slowing significantly or ceasing entirely on many measures of educational success.[3] For example, blacks' math achievement test scores remained steady after the late 1980s; in reading, black students made modest gains from 1975 to the mid 1980s, but then lost ground. Disparities between black and white school-age children in these basic skills remain great, with black children in fourth to twelfth grades testing between 0.8 and 1 standard deviation behind whites on the National Assessment of Educational Progress (NAEP) in this decade. As summarized by economist Derek Neal, "overall, black-white math and reading gaps in 2004 among 9- to 13-year-olds are quite similar to the gaps observed in the late 1980s."[4] Disparities by race among school-age children persist into the teenage years, with recent SAT scores revealing a large and widening gap. In 2003, the average combined scores for incoming college freshmen (who represent the most able group among all test-takers) were 1063 for whites and 1083 for Asians, as compared with 857 for blacks and 905 for Mexican-Americans. The overall 206-point white-black gap in 2003 is up from 187 points in 1993.[5] A substantial difference in the scores of blacks and whites, representing one standard deviation, is also found on the Armed Forces Qualification Test (AFQT), a test of cognitive skills administered to military recruits.[6] Average score differences mask more pronounced disparities among top scorers, with little or no recent improvement in black underrepresentation among the most able contingent of test-takers.[7] Blacks also lag in educational attainment. In a study conducted in 2000, 34 percent of whites received at least a bachelor's degree, as compared with 17 percent of blacks.[8]

Why have gaps stopped closing or even widened, and why do significant disparities remain? The potential explanations divide roughly into two types: those that look to external factors independent of, and beyond the immediate control of, the students and families—what social scientists call exogenous factors—and those that, although influenced by external circumstances, are caught up with the behavioral choices of students and their parents. These are sometimes designated as endogenous factors because the endpoints being measured (such as student learning, achievement, or completed years of schooling) are not solely the product of external forces. Rather, they are substantially within the control of the subjects themselves.

Economists and sociologists have long linked racial disparities in educational outcomes to socioeconomic factors such as parental education and resources. In general, students from more affluent and higher-status families outscore those who are poor, and black families are on average less affluent and educated than others. The precise mechanism through which family background differences produce disparate student achievement is contested, with some researchers emphasizing family resources and others pointing to child-rearing practices that correlate with income and education. But regardless of how the observed gaps actually arise, it is now well documented that differences in family income and education fail to explain most of the black-white achievement gap. Significant racial disparities exist even among students with similar economic backgrounds. Black students from families earning more than $70,000 per year have lower SAT scores than white students from families with less than $30,000 in income. White students with parents who are high school graduates outscore black students whose parents attended or graduated from college. These data indicate that a significant portion of blacks' poor educational performance is not due to poverty or parents' lack of education.[9]

Likewise, the theory that observed racial differences stem from institutional failures, such as poor schools, unequal educational spending, or lack of funds for higher education, does not hold up well despite voluminous attempts to link these variables with deficits in learning. School quality is often invoked to explain the race achievement gap. This is a slippery concept that can encompass a range of factors, including caliber of instruction, expenditures per pupil, and student socioeconomic background, that are sometimes hard to measure and that operate through a variety of mechanisms. In particular, it is important to recognize that a school's quality is not wholly a function of exogenous variables. Rather, it depends critically on endogenous elements, such as the characteristics, behavior, and education-related attitudes of the students themselves. These very factors are notoriously resistant to outside manipulation.

There is evidence that, in some limited respects, the schools that blacks attend are not quite as good as those in which whites are enrolled. In general, however, measured differences are small and of uncertain or undocumented importance to outcomes. Overall, there is little reason to believe that black students' schools are significantly inferior on the parameters that have been demonstrated to matter to quality of education. Along traditional dimensions of school quality (such as class size, student-teacher ratios, curriculum, and computer resources), the schools that blacks and whites attend became more similar during the 1980s and 1990s and now differ little on average.[10] To be sure, expenditures per pupil tend to track average family income, which varies by district. These resource differences mean that schools in districts with many poor (and black) students tend to be somewhat more crowded, older, less well maintained, and less varied in course offerings.[11] Nonetheless, some majority black city districts spend heavily on their public schools, so expenditures per pupil are similar by race overall, with the average per-student amount for whites actually lower than for nonwhites.[12] In general, however, the relationship between spending and learning is not well established, and research has failed to demonstrate a clear link.[13] Between 1972 and 1992, when increased state-level spending significantly reduced interdistrict disparities, race gaps in test scores consistently failed to narrow.[14]

Likewise, key factors that affect the classroom experience do not seem to explain black-white differences in attainment. From the 1970s through the 1990s, teacher quality (as measured by teachers' educational background, quality of schools attended, and qualifications for subject of teaching) deteriorated across the board in all school districts, regardless of affluence and racial composition. Although poor and nonwhite districts improved relative to whiter and wealthier districts in teacher-to-student ratios, they continued to lag somewhat in teacher training and experience.[15] The differences were not large, however, and none of these variables has been reliably linked to student outcomes.

Researchers have also sought to examine other institutional variables that might bear on learning but are ordinarily not captured in standard studies of school quality. They have attempted for decades to investigate the claim that low teacher expectations depress black student achievement. The theory is that low expectations create "self-fulfilling prophecies": If teachers expect black students to do poorly, students respond by failing to achieve and learn. But the literature fails to demonstrate that self-fulfilling prophecies depress black achievement.[16] In the few studies suggesting that lower expectations might influence minority children, measured effects are "small, fragile, and fleeting."[17] In addition, most research in this area suffers from the serious methodological flaw of failing to distinguish between low teacher expectations as a cause of black students' poor performance or as a response to those students' actual underachievement.[18]

Yet another hypothesis attributes low black achievement to a race mismatch of students and teachers: Students do poorly because they lack role models or because their teachers don't understand or respond to their learning style. There is little support for this view. Although one recent Tennessee study detects somewhat better performance by students with same-race teachers, the authors themselves admit that the effects have "at best been limited and qualified."[19] Overall, empirical studies have found little or no evidence that being taught by black teachers raises black student achievement.

In a similar vein, achievement differences by race are frequently blamed on the effects of "stereotype threat." The theory is that black students fall short because they are afraid tests and other performance measures will be used to confirm negative views about their group's abilities. Despite much publicity, the impact of stereotype threat has been greatly exaggerated. There is currently no evidence that the effects attributed to stereotype threat account for more than a negligible portion of the overall black-white gap in achievement and test scores.[20]

In sum, the data reveal that the schools black children attend lag a bit on some measures of school quality, such as teacher experience, physical condition of the school, and number of advanced or enrichment courses, but are better on others, including student-teacher ratios and spending per student. The measured effects are not large in either direction. The key questions are whether these observed disparities are the driving force behind racial gaps in achievement and whether there is reason to believe that erasing these differences (if that could be achieved) would eliminate existing discrepancies in student performance.

The critical issue is whether the observed minor differences in schooling quality are causing the present significant gaps in educational achievement. For teacher training and certification, for example, one study found that predominantly minority schools have 7.6 percent fewer teachers with master's degrees than schools with mostly nonminority students.[21] But the significance of even that small disparity is questionable: Most studies show little or no connection between teacher certification and student learning. Similarly, teachers in predominantly black schools tend to have somewhat less teaching experience. But the effect of small differences in experience has not been well established.[22] Although there is evidence that teachers do vary in qualities that affect student learning, research also shows that measurable credentials (such as possession of a master's degree or years of teaching) are poor proxies for good teaching. Rather, there is general agreement that direct classroom monitoring is needed to assess teacher quality.[23] But reliable, large-scale, observational information about what teachers actually do in their classrooms is not currently available, so there is as yet no basis for attributing the black-white achievement gap to poor teaching.

Deficits in Employment

Blacks and whites differ in employment rates, earnings, and occupational attainment. Although racial gaps in workplace success narrowed after World War II and the enactment of civil rights legislation, progress has slowed or stalled in recent decades. Discrimination is often cited as an important cause of lingering disparities. Yet, social scientists and economists have increasingly turned their attention to so-called supply-side factors—those bearing on job performance and the development of human capital. The list of proposed sources of such deficits includes resource constraints (such as insufficient funds for higher education and underfinancing of schools), private endowments and inputs (such as inadequate parental investments in children), and personal behaviors (such as criminal activity, lack of academic self-development, and choices reflecting poor socialization or work ethic).

A consensus has now emerged in labor economics that supply-side deficits account for almost all remaining racial disparities in employment outcomes. Much of the racial gap in jobs and earnings can be traced to differences in learning and academic achievement. A recent summary states unequivocally that "black-white skills gaps are the driving force behind black-white differences in labor market outcomes among adults."[24] Investigations of the contribution to job outcomes of various human capital inputs—including cognitive skill, educational achievement, and actual learning—yield a remarkably consistent picture: Personal and behavioral attributes related to productivity are by far the most important predictors of job market success, regardless of race.[25] Most studies reveal that blacks and whites with similar levels of cognitive skill (as measured by tests of intelligence and educational aptitude) and educational attainment (as measured by quantity and quality of education, basic math and reading proficiency, and overall learning) receive similar job market rewards, including salaries and promotions.[26] Where unexplained racial disparities persist, they are typically small and fail to apply across the board. Although the data do not rule out the possibility that these residual differences are due to old-fashioned discrimination, other factors—such as poor job networking, geographic mismatch, and disparities in degree and type of work experience—could also explain the observed results.[27] Moreover, whereas less-educated black men lag a bit behind their white counterparts in earnings, black male college graduates earn as much or more than white college graduates of similar aptitude. All in all, there is little evidence that observed job market patterns are due to discrimination. Skill, ability, experience, and productivity count far more.

Poorer job outcomes and the expectation of job market discrimination are sometimes cited as a cause of lower educational achievement in blacks. One contention is that blacks' failure to invest in education is a rational strategy because employers can be expected to undervalue their skills.[28] The data show that this logic is flawed. Because "the relationship between basic skills and eventual earnings is stronger among black men than white men," and because earnings grow faster for blacks than whites as educational level increases, blacks have every reason to stay in school and invest in self-development.[29] Although black men may harbor and act on the belief that they are discriminated against in the job market, the evidence reveals that this reaction is unjustified and dysfunctional. Failing to pursue an education is not a rational response to actual patterns of labor market rewards.

To be sure, the econometric findings do not mean that racial discrimination has altogether disappeared. There are some data suggesting that employers are leery of less-educated blacks, especially men. For example, employers tend to hire white over black ex-convicts[30] and to disfavor job candidates with black-sounding names.[31] Studies with job testers reveal a mild preference in some markets for white job candidates over blacks with similar objective credentials.[32] In general, however, studies like these involve small samples of subjects. In contrast, econometric analyses showing that discrimination is minimal examine large population trends. In addition, the effects attributed to discrimination, even in these smaller-scale studies, are modest. They often barely reach statistical significance.

The patterns of residual racial disparity are often suggestive of so-called rational or statistical discrimination.[33] Statistical discrimination represents an employer's response to real average gaps in performance between members of different groups. When groups differ systematically in productivity-related skills or behaviors and it is difficult or expensive to observe individual characteristics directly, employers may use group attributes such as race as a proxy for job-related traits. If the average black male performs less well than the average white with apparently similar credentials, employers may "read between the lines" to devalue all black male employees, regardless of individual ability to do the job.

Because easily measured qualifications, such as years of schooling, are not entirely reliable indicators of actual knowledge or skill, statistical discrimination can be a cost-effective, albeit imperfect, strategy for screening prospective employees. Paper credentials sometimes mask real racial differences relevant to job performance. For example, blacks graduate from high school with markedly lower average reading and math test scores than whites.[34] This evidence suggests that, for jobs that draw on academic ability, blacks are on average less qualified than whites with similar years of education. There may also be group-related differences in noncognitive or "soft" attributes—such as social skills, work-related attitudes, or elements of social background (including family structure and stability of personal relationships)—that may influence or correlate with productivity but are not always revealed by conventional screening methods. Although there is some evidence of racial differences along these lines, behavioral contrasts of this type can be hard to demonstrate systematically.[35] Nonetheless, many employers harbor the perception that soft skills are not uniform by race.[36] Such perceptions may lead employers to disfavor blacks generally or to be wary of distinct subgroups, such as black ex-convicts or those with black-sounding names. The situation is complicated by the fact that race in our society correlates with social or economic background, which, regardless of paper credentials, is linked with job-related behaviors. In fact, persons with distinctly black names tend to come from less educated and less affluent homes, and there is evidence that employers are sensitive to this.[37]

Statistical discrimination, when and if it occurs, does pose an obstacle to employment by making the struggle for economic success even harder for blacks. Nonetheless, the impact of this phenomenon, by any measure, is small. The data fail to reveal a significant role for this sort of rational discrimination or for discrimination of any kind. Even if some racial differences in job outcomes remain unexplained, it is far from clear that race-based discrimination, as opposed to other factors, account for them. Employers may not be using race at all. Rather, they may be responding *directly* to so-called "unobservable" or "hidden" variables—that is, real differences in credentials or productivity-related attributes that are apparent to managers or supervisors and that correlate with race but are difficult for social scientists to assess. In any event, investigations of employer bias focus almost exclusively on the screening and hiring stages. There is virtually no hard evidence that race-based generalizations affect decisions about pay raises or job advancement. And there is even less reason to believe that statistical discrimination would come into play for those decisions because evaluations of existing employees are based on a richer body of information, including direct observations of on-the-job performance, than is available at initial hiring.

Deficits in Family Structure and Home Environment

The black family has long been in disarray. Compared with whites and other races, blacks marry less often, divorce more, and have far higher rates of extramarital childbearing.[38] Yet the situation was not always so dire. Earlier in the twentieth century, black marriage rates were high and extramarital childbearing was the exception. That did not last. Although the postwar years have seen periods of black progress on other fronts, the black family has steadily deteriorated.

The growth in family structure differences by race has occurred against a background of divergence by education and economic class.[39] Although marriage rates have declined for all sociodemographic groups, the trend is most pronounced among the poor and least skilled. Class differences are particularly stark among whites, with the affluent and well educated still marrying and staying married at high rates. In contrast, marriage has become less common among blacks in every social class, with the steepest decline among poorer blacks.[40] Overall, marriage rates are significantly lower, and divorce and extramarital birth rates higher, for blacks than for whites at all levels of education and income.

One consequence of these patterns is that relatively fewer black adults and children reap the benefits of living in stable, conventional nuclear families. In particular, the decline in marriage among blacks has important implications for the setting in which children grow up. Today there are many more black than white children living with only one parent. Although fractured and fatherless families prevail among the poor, they are also common among middle-class blacks. Overall, more than two-thirds of black children are born out of wedlock. Multiple-partner fertility—or the practice of having children by more than one partner—is significantly more common among blacks than other American ethnic groups, and more often involves extramarital children.[41] In contrast, about one-quarter of white children are born to unmarried mothers, with almost all such births in this group confined to low-income and less-educated women. Very few white women with a college degree bear children outside of marriage, and relatively few become single mothers through divorce.[42]

Do blacks' low rate of marriage and higher rate of out-of-wedlock childbearing matter? These patterns have important consequences because family structure is linked to deficits that hold blacks back. A growing body of research shows that children who grow up with single or unmarried parents are less well-off on many measures. In addition to having lower educational achievement and completing fewer years of schooling, they experience more behavioral and psychological problems throughout life and have less stable adult relationships.[43] This is partly due to fewer resources: Single parent and nonmarital families have less money than families headed by married couples. But these effects are also observed when parents are matched for income and education. That is, growing up without two married parents in itself produces worse outcomes.[44] The relatively high rates of divorce and cohabitation among blacks also add to risks for children. Recent research suggests that children do best when raised by married, biological parents and that children in blended or step-parent families fare no better than children raised by comparable single or divorced parents.[45] Households with biologically unrelated males are particularly detrimental for children.[46]

Although social scientists disagree on how much black family fragility contributes to educational and labor market disparities by race, the consensus is growing that its influence is significant. Building on prior work by economist James Heckman, Derek Neal identifies black-white differences in early childhood experiences as a critical cause of persistent racial gaps in labor market outcomes.[47] Family structure is thought to affect investments in children. These investments in turn contribute to cognitive as well as noncognitive attributes that are crucial to educational attainment and job success.[48] Black family structure and reproductive patterns also harm children indirectly by weakening neighborhoods and communities. Responsible, married fathers are exceptional, and resident biological fathers are uncommon even among the black middle class. The absence of fathers undermines the supervision and proper socialization of children, and loosely attached adult males create a potentially disruptive presence.

In sum, the evidence suggests that the continuing deterioration of the black family has contributed significantly to widening disparities in economic position and human capital development between blacks and other racial groups. Nonetheless, fractured families are only one source of racial gaps in human capital development that bear on economic success. Cultural differences in parenting practices also appear to play a role.[49] Although black children on average come from poorer and less-educated homes, significant racial differences in children's school readiness and subsequent performance are observed even for families with similar income, parental education, and family structure. In attempting to account for these differences, social scientists have investigated such factors as home environment and routines, parental behavior, children's activities, and family attitudes toward learning. Findings suggest that young black children are exposed to lower levels of cognitive and emotional stimulation than whites and Asians, even in families matched for income, education, and IQ. Black children watch more TV, read fewer books, are taken on educational outings less often, and are subjected to more erratic routines. Developmental research on these elements of upbringing, although not definitive, suggests they are important predictors of lifelong outcomes.[50] Although measured differences by race are reflected most immediately in school readiness and performance, they have potential consequences beyond the childhood years for adult social adjustment and occupational success.

The conclusion that home environment and private social life exert a pivotal influence finds additional support in a growing body of literature on the relationship between noncognitive attributes and life outcomes. Although achievement in school is important to economic position, the evidence suggests that neither educational attainment nor subsequent occupational success depends exclusively on cognitive skills. Also crucial are noncognitive aspects of personality and character, including industriousness, perseverance, trustworthiness, honesty, cooperativeness, agreeableness, conscientiousness, and future orientation.[51] These traits predict school success and also translate into the "soft skills" that employers seek. These same characteristics may be important to staying out of trouble with the law and to the ability to sustain an orderly, harmonious, and stable family life.

There is some evidence for a race gap in these noncognitive attributes. Black students outscore whites, even controlling for socioeconomic background, on some measures of anti-social behaviors.[52] In one study, a preemployment screening personality test administered by a large American company revealed differences by race, with blacks scoring lower on two key noncognitive attributes, agreeableness and conscientiousness, that the employer at issue deemed desirable.[53]

Why might these types of traits be unevenly distributed? There has been relatively little attention paid to date to the origins of those noncognitive skills that are most crucial to life success. More research is needed to identify the attributes, habits, inclinations, and behaviors that contribute to effective performance and to determine how best to foster them. Existing evidence suggests, however, that families are vital to proper socialization. Private, informal institutions have proved most effective in inculcating these characteristics.[54]

Across the board, the social science reveals that observed racial differentials in educational attainment, economic position, and labor market outcomes no longer can be ascribed to the "usual suspects." First and foremost, there is no straightforward relationship between present, ongoing discrimination based on race and observed patterns, and thus little reason to believe that eliminating such discrimination will work a significant change. This does not entail denying a connection between current patterns and past oppression. But the fact that persistent shortfalls are the outgrowth of past mistreatment tells us little about how current inequalities can effectively be erased. The critical question for our purposes remains: What does this analysis imply for remedies? How are disparities in educational achievement, employment, and family environment best addressed?

Education Remedies

Although the schools that blacks attend lag in some measures of quality, they are equal or better in others. Differences in school spending and resources are generally too small and variable to account for large and pervasive racial gaps in test scores and skills. Observed institutional deficits are, on average, modest and often of unproven significance. Teachers of black students are somewhat less experienced, but studies to date have not reliably linked experience to teacher effectiveness and student learning. There is little evidence that teachers expect less of their minority students or that such expectations affect performance. Also, the data fail to show that stereotype threat has more than a negligible impact relative to the overall gap in test scores and proficiency.

In light of these observations, what promise does ridding the system of differences in school quality really hold for closing gaps in achievement and outcomes? If all disparities in the average schooling experience of blacks and whites could be eliminated, would racial differences in academic outcomes disappear? Would they even measurably shrink? There is currently no basis for thinking so. Although pursuing equity in schools may be justified as a matter of fairness, that strategy does not hold much promise for closing observed racial gaps in academic performance.

It might be that standard measures of quality, which focus on facilities, teachers, and broad resources, fail to capture what really matters. There are documented racial differences in such "nonstandard" school inputs as gang problems, violence and fighting, drug use or drug dealing, disruptive and uncooperative students, the number of learning-disabled students, students receiving free lunch, the safety of the school neighborhood, or loitering near schools by nonstudents.[55] These factors may influence student achievement. But the problem with these factors is that they are fundamentally different from the resource measures central to standard school assessments. These elements are overwhelmingly "endogenous":

they reflect demographic characteristics of the school and its surrounding community and are inextricably linked to the attitudes and behaviors of students and their families. The same point applies to other parameters—including time spent on schoolwork and homework, respect for teachers, obedience, order, cooperation in the classroom, and fellow students' academic interests. Students learn more if they are surrounded by peers who are studious, intellectually serious, and ambitious.[56] Such peer qualities may differ by school or may vary among groups of students in the same school. All these attributes may correlate with race. But if such factors are critical to outcomes, it is difficult to know what to do about them. The atmosphere in school is a function of how the students themselves approach school. That atmosphere depends on students' behavior, preferences, and outlook. No known school reform to date has succeeded in transforming how students think about education and learning. More importantly, school policies cannot change the deep-seated attitude that education is something delivered rather than actively acquired.[57] Education is an individual responsibility, and each student is the gatekeeper of his or her own educational success. Progress depends on each student's effort and discipline. Despite wishful thinking to the contrary, educating those who are not ready and willing to learn is not a project readily amenable to policy initiatives.[58]

Perhaps the most persuasive evidence that manipulating what goes on in schools will not do much to close the black-white achievement gap comes from observing the performance of students within the *same* schools. By definition, such comparisons factor out most disparities in school conditions, except perhaps those that might exist between classrooms. Yet even within the same school, Asians and whites consistently outscore blacks on most important measures of educational achievement. These racial differences remain even for students with similar backgrounds, as measured by parental income and years of education.[59] Researchers who examine group performance within schools posit various behavioral or cultural explanations for these differences. These include blacks' lower levels of effort in class, less time spent on homework, less extracurricular reading, and an antipathy to "acting white" or embracing what are perceived as white norms of intellectual accomplishment.[60] In addition, as noted, there is evidence that black, white, and Asian families differ in parenting practices and a range of other domestic patterns of behavior that have been shown to correlate with achievement.

Yet another observation that points away from the power of school reform to eliminate or even significantly reduce inequalities in educational outcomes is that large racial gaps open up early, before students even arrive at school. Several independent studies have documented that black students entering kindergarten lag significantly behind white students in school readiness, vocabulary, and math.[61] Disparities tend to widen as children age and progress through school.[62] These differences persist even among students from two-parent families with similar levels of education and income. That large differences show up in young, preschool children indicates that race gaps in achievement and cognitive attainment do not originate at school. In addition, early disparities belie the contention that black underachievement can be traced to low teacher expectations or students' response to discrimination in the classroom, since young black children show deficits before discrimination could have much effect.

That factors such as family structure, home environment, and informal social expectations are more important to educational success than what happens in school is not a new observation.[63] Children's cognitive and noncognitive attributes originate in private experiences that have deep cultural roots. The behaviors and outlooks that bear most directly on adult performance are learned early and there is little indication that, once children reach school age, institutional initiatives or educational interventions can significantly alter them.

Given these insights, what are the remedies for observed racial disparities in educational outcomes? One popular and frequently voiced recommendation is to drastically improve the quality and skill of teachers. If only excellent teachers could be lured to lagging schools, it is suggested, significant progress could be made.[64] On this view, how students themselves approach their education should be no obstacle. Teachers who encounter unruly, disrespectful, or indifferent students must respond by making learning relevant and appealing. They must be trained to manage or even transform student attitudes and behavior. These suggestions blink reality. Good teachers are understandably reluctant to teach unprepared and undisciplined students, especially where their authority is undermined by an administrative commitment to keeping everyone in the classroom. They resent being held accountable for learning deficits and behavioral problems that are not of their own making and not within their control. Higher pay is unlikely to compensate for these aspects of the job. Likewise, the idea that better teaching techniques can elicit cooperation or negate student indifference sounds good in theory but rarely works in practice. Expecting teachers to accomplish these tasks is unrealistic and is a formula for driving the most qualified teachers away. But the real problem with the focus on teacher quality is that there is no reason to believe that more qualified teachers and better teaching can produce the needed boost in learning under current conditions. Teachers simply cannot accomplish what is asked of them without a fundamental change in the students themselves.

Another proposed solution to racial gaps in educational attainment is to increase blacks' relatively low rates of college attendance and graduation. Blacks are not as affluent as whites, and their lack of money would appear to be an important impediment to access to higher education. New public and private financing programs have been proposed as the solution. Yet there is little evidence that money is the rate-limiting step in black college attendance and graduation. Rather, as economists Pedro Carneiro and James Heckman have shown, virtually all black students who are well prepared for college can find the funds to attend.[65] Financial aid and loans are widely available for students who are qualified, and whites and blacks with the same test scores in eighth grade are equally likely to receive an undergraduate degree.[66] These data indicate that black college attendance is low because too few students are academically prepared to do college-level work. These deficits are, once again, rooted in earlier educational failure, which in turn is predominantly due to "the influence of family factors present from birth through adolescence."[67] Interest in college, willingness to take on debt, family support, determination, persistence, and personal organization, which are all conditioned by attitudes and cultural background, surely play a role, although there is little reliable data on these. Nonetheless, the existing evidence does point to shortfalls in cognitive and noncognitive attributes, rather than lack of money or the inability to borrow, as the most important impediments to college attendance. Likewise, prior educational preparation and attainment are the most critical factors influencing college graduation rates. Although some poor students, put off by high costs and the complications of applying for aid, may fail to enroll despite the availability of funds, there is no reason to believe that significant numbers of otherwise able students are deterred for this reason. Finances cannot be regarded as a significant obstacle to black college attendance because aid is widely available to well-prepared students regardless of race or income. Yet these insights have failed to influence policymakers, as evidenced by recent proposals to expand public funding and extend tax credits to help pay for college.[68]

The insistence that better teachers are the solution to racial gaps in learning, or that more funding is critical to higher black college attendance, illustrates a larger pattern in approaches to racial disadvantage across the board. The temptation is to see problems as amenable to programmatic solutions and to focus on "brick-wall" obstacles that can be removed through external interventions. Teacher quality appears more tractable than the behavior and determination of students themselves. Lack of money is far easier to address than students' inability to compete or complete academic requirements. Yet the problem of black underachievement is a matter not of surmounting brick walls, but rather of taking on the hard struggles that undermine performance.

It may be argued that a focus on open access and equal opportunity misses the point. Fundamental remedial principles teach us that making room for those who can and will do the work does not suffice. We must be prepared to go well beyond that. Whatever is causing students to start out and lag behind must be addressed institutionally. Society must commit ever more money to closing existing gaps in academic and personal skills. Whatever it takes is what is required. Without that, justice will not be done. Extraordinary efforts will surely be needed not just to make the school experience for blacks equivalent but to make it far better than for other races. If deficits occur before students get to school, then new initiatives must be devised, both within schools and in addition to schools, to address them. Even if families, communities, and culture are the immediate source of the problem, the government must intervene to undo what those influences have wrought. The efforts must go above and beyond what has ever been done before. They cannot cease until the problem is solved.

As a matter of remedial imperatives, this position is compelling. Justice demands this approach. But will such initiatives actually succeed? Once again, dispelling the notion that more resources and new programs will produce the desired result requires proving a negative. It can never be definitively established that such efforts won't work. But sustained experience and experimentation, including decades of social programs directed at these problems, provide ample reason to doubt they ever will. Some insist that nothing short of heroic upgrades—such as sharp increases in teacher quality or the drastic revamping of all school programs, will suffice. Unfortunately, these types of transformations are not feasible on a wide scale, even with unlimited expenditures.[69] Yet even if these dramatic changes could be made, there is no basis for believing they would make a real difference. Once again, the faith in extraordinary reforms is grounded in remedial idealism. The possibility that, as with the injured pedestrian, the effectiveness of outside help may have reached its limits, or that the victim's own efforts have become the rate-limiting step, is deemed unthinkable.

Perhaps the most popular proposal across the political spectrum is for the creation of universal, well-funded, intensive, preschool programs to address children's intellectual, social, and emotional development.[70] In response to evidence that disadvantaged children develop critical deficits before entering school, these proposals often include training and coaching for lower-class and minority parents.[71] To date, several such initiatives, including Head Start and the Perry Preschool Project, have been tried. Although these programs have generally failed to boost cognitive ability as reflected in IQ scores, some have produced small but measurable reductions in adult anti-social behaviors like crime and chronic unemployment.[72] The resulting modest economic benefits may make these programs worth undertaking.[73]

It is nonetheless legitimate to ask whether a truly enduring solution to the long-term problems faced by blacks lies with large-scale public investments in early childhood and parental education programs. Because any expected effects will be small relative to the overall magnitude of the problem, even a strong public policy push in this area will not make a significant dent. The question is not whether society as a whole should take on the task of alleviating or making up for early learning deficits. Rather, it is whether a massive redirection of public resources to early childhood programs can actually succeed in transforming child-rearing practices, or, alternatively, in fully compensating for their effects.

Addressing this question requires facing up to the fact that the influence of families, communities, and culture dwarfs other factors. It may be society's duty to improve on or compensate for early experiences, but the fact remains that we know how to do neither. Experience shows that governments are virtually powerless in this arena. No programmatic intervention can control how parents interact with children or influence community behaviors that are critical to children's upbringing. The government cannot make people watch less television, talk to their children, or read more books. It cannot ordain domestic order, harmony, tranquility, stability, or other conditions conducive to academic success and the development of sound character. Nor can it determine how families structure their interactions and routines or how family resources—including time and money—are expended. Large-scale programs are especially ineffective in changing attitudes and values toward learning, work, and marriage. Likewise, special programs, including intensive preschool projects described above, have not found ways to make up for deficiencies in the home environment. Many different interventions have been tried, but none so far has done much to negate suboptimal behaviors or erase their effects. It is always tempting to respond that "We need to try harder, keep searching, devote more resources and spend more money." This exhortation ignores that, given what we know, the ability of society to take effective action is limited.

Is there another way? There is. All evidence shows that the most powerful influence on children's life chances is the home environment. Given the family's and the community's immediate contribution to racial disparities, and the longstanding inadequacy of institutional alternatives, private initiatives appear to be far more important than programmatic reforms. Changes in group behavior, attitudes, and child-rearing practices are the most promising avenue for closing existing gaps.

The approach that proceeds from this insight is radical. It requires accepting that there is no policy solution to observed racial gaps in academic achievement. It requires giving up on institutional fixes. This does not mean that improvement is impossible. As with the parable of the pedestrian, the way forward requires accepting that the victims' decisions and conduct are now the rate-limiting step, that the solution lies with them if it lies anywhere, and that self-correction is the only available *effective* strategy. Families must recognize that they have primary and dominant control over how children are reared. Parents and those in their social circle must make their own habits and practices their chief, if not their exclusive, focus. They must examine these with a critical eye and figure out how to change them. Although community institutions and organizations must work with and support parents in their efforts, they should not pretend they can substitute or compensate for untoward private conduct.

Embarking on such a self-help project is not easy to do. And as discussed more extensively below, changing behavior on a wide enough scale to make a difference poses a formidable challenge of collective action. Impediments are both psychological and informational. One issue that has bedeviled efforts to tackle race and class differentials is the possibility that racial differences in IQ are inherited. As measured by standard IQ tests, blacks on average have lower cognitive ability than whites or Asians.[74] Although the very suggestion that group cognitive differences are even partly based in biology is verboten in popular and academic discourse, the science on this question is inconclusive.[75] At this point it is not known whether different groups are equally endowed with all the abilities that make for success in modern technological societies. And even apart from this, not everyone is equipped for high academic achievement.[76] But none of this rules out significant room for improvement.

The evidence is strong that the environment—familial and cultural—exerts a major influence on cognitive ability, character, and learning.[77] And a consensus has emerged that early childhood is a crucial period of development for later life success. Despite decades of investigation, however, much remains unknown about how specific childrearing practices, cultural values, and other environmental influences affect children's development. It is unclear what aspects of upbringing are most important and whether or how they can be effectively manipulated.[78] Although it is known that children's outcomes correlate with socioeconomic status and race, for example, the bases for these differentials are not completely understood, and observed correlations do not reveal the precise mechanisms through which some families and their children do better.

Despite the unknowns, fully tackling the problem of race requires confronting the evidence that family wealth and resources, though important, are not everything. Black children underperform at every level of family education and income. And the data also show that these effects cannot be explained through conventional, external mechanisms of oppression or blocked opportunity. Detailed, sustained, and impartial investigations of the private influences that promote educational and occupational success are therefore essential. Efforts should be directed at identifying the cultural patterns, attitudes, and practices that produce differential outcomes by race.

Above all, rejecting programmatic solutions should not be seen as giving up, and existing deficits should not be viewed as destiny. Although money and race now predict outcomes, the measures needed to promote children's success are not inherently inaccessible to less privileged families. Nor are minority families doomed to underachievement. That families with modest means, few advantages, and insular lives do create environments conducive to children's good behavior, learning, and success shows that this goal is within the reach of a broad range of people from disparate backgrounds.[79] Whether and how these successes can be generalized remains to be seen. More specifically, whether the needed cultural sea change can be effected remains an open and vexed question.[80] But common sense suggests that the most important steps are not expensive and are readily amenable to self-help. Reading books and turning off the television take effort, but don't cost much (and can actually save money). Achieving quiet and order at home are within the power of ordinary people of modest means. Adopting a serious attitude toward learning and spending more time on educational pursuits is likewise within reach. Finally, getting married before having children is not expensive and actually improves economic status.

What is required is a wholehearted belief in the necessity of making changes like these and the fervent determination to do so. Nothing short of a new self-help movement will do.

Employment Remedies

A similar analysis applies to deficits in employment. The chief obstacles to equality in this sphere are not the "brick walls" that dominated in past periods. They are not the hard and fast impediments of exclusion or discrimination based on race. Rather, individuals today face the struggle of developing the skills and human capital necessary to succeed in a society which, despite its imperfections, offers many opportunities to progress and achieve a decent life.

As already discussed, data collected and analyzed by labor economists in recent years show that race-based discrimination accounts for, at most, a negligible portion of the disadvantage blacks suffer in the labor market. In his comprehensive review of the literature on black-white differences in employment outcomes, Derek Neal concludes that shortfalls in cognitive and noncognitive attributes drive most disparities.[81] Neal also notes that, even after controlling for standard influences on human capital formation (such as parental income and years of schooling), there are still significant differences by race in the capabilities employers seek. He attributes these to forms of parenting and upbringing that depend on group practices and cultural norms.

There is widespread resistance to the notion that shortfalls in skill and human capital formation are critical to persistent race disparities in the workplace. Likewise, few accept that these shortcomings are largely a function of cultural influence rather than of ongoing discrimination, material deprivation, lack of educational opportunity, or other concrete barriers to self-improvement. Nonetheless, the evidence belies the received wisdom. The data clearly indicate that individuals are not taking full advantage of the opportunities presented.

The insistence that discrimination is still pervasive and accounts for observed outcomes often rests on the claim that most workplace bias no longer takes the form of wrongful, intentional acts of exclusion or injury by identifiable discriminators. Rather, group-based disadvantage is now the product of "second-generation" discrimination.[82] On this theory, women and minorities face systematic disadvantages in training, mentoring, assignments, and assessment "fueled by stereotypes about [them] that are incompatible with the image of the ideal worker."[83] This type of discrimination "seldom involves a conscious decision to exclude or subordinate," but rather represents the cumulative effects of unconscious stereotyping.[84] Proponents of this view rely heavily on a body of work in experimental psychology that purports to demonstrate that individuals tend to generalize about groups. In particular, commentators point to a laboratory test of split-second mental association, the Implicit Association Test (or IAT), which shows that many people are quicker to link negative concepts, such as poverty or crime, with blacks than with whites.[85]

Claims based on unconscious stereotyping are amorphous and sweeping.[86] First, reliance on the IAT and other laboratory tests of implicit bias is misplaced because it rests on dubious assumptions. One is that everyone who "flunks" the IAT harbors negative attitudes and endorses negative stereotypes about minorities. Another is that people who show split-second negative associations on the IAT will discriminate in everyday decisions and judgments affecting others. Neither of those conclusions is justified. Implicit negative associations are as compatible with positive attitudes toward minorities as with hostile ones. People with very different political and personal views could easily harbor mental constructs based on awareness of existing social patterns (such as the undeniable fact that blacks are more likely to be incarcerated or poor) or on exposure to socially prevalent stereotypes.[87] Thus, mere knowledge of the troubled state of the black community could trigger the observed linkage of black faces with negative concepts. Second, thinking is not acting and brain states are not behavior. People can respond to their own mental associations—whether conscious or unconscious—in many different ways. The few behavioral studies that exist suggest that IAT results do not reliably predict actual discriminatory behavior.[88] Indeed, some people who score high on IAT bias measures are even observed to bend over backwards in favor of minorities instead of acting against them. In addition, there is good evidence that people often ignore stereotypes if they possess more detailed "counter-stereotypical" information about persons they know well, such as those they work with every day.[89]

More importantly, however, "second wave" discrimination theory makes the unwarranted assumption that disparities in outcome by race necessarily spell discrimination. In failing to carefully consider alternative supply side explanations, the second-wave literature virtually ignores the large body of data showing that inputs matter: individuals with similar cognitive ability, educational credentials, and experience achieve similar earnings and positions regardless of race. This literature indicates that disparate outcomes are not best explained by demand-side institutional defects or inadvertent biases. Rather, they are almost entirely due to supply side deficits in individual skills or behaviors employers value. That employment markets are highly responsive to real group differences in hard and soft skills suggests that employers' paramount interest is in finding good workers and rewarding actual productivity. Overwhelmingly, regardless of race, what determines workplace success is performance and ability to do the job. In the long run, labor markets are remarkably faithful to these outcome-based priorities.

The evidence, however, does not definitively rule out some minor role for so-called rational or statistical discrimination. As already discussed, employers' reluctance to hire individual black workers might be motivated by concerns about lower groups productivity or other characteristics that may not be fully revealed by standard qualifications based on race. This type of race-based discrimination is hard to demonstrate because it mimics a response to actual job-related characteristics. Nonetheless, the practice of rational discrimination, if it exists, would make it harder for even highly skilled black workers to be hired. Assuming there remains some residual discrimination of this type, the most important issue is how it is best addressed.

Title VII forbids race-based discrimination against individuals even if grounded in valid generalizations or real average group differences. Discrimination of any kind is illegal and must be met by vigorous enforcement of anti-discrimination laws. Unfortunately, legal sanctions against statistical discrimination are cumbersome and of limited effectiveness. Because this practice picks up on real group-related performance differences, it is difficult to prove that observed workplace disparities are due to this type of discrimination. And unlike animus-based bias, screening in response to real group differences may be cost-effective for employers overall despite the exclusion of some workers who could perform well. As a cheap, quick, and dirty way to winnow out less productive employees, valid group-based generalizations are hard to root out.

But there is an alternative approach: The most effective and enduring solution to rational discrimination is to render it irrational. By definition, employers who engage in this type of discrimination are responding to real average differences in productivity. But if underperforming groups catch up, the rationale for employer bias will vanish as well. This suggests that statistical discrimination is best tackled by negating its preconditions—the actual group disparities that underlie racial generalizations. To be sure, such generalizations will not disappear overnight. Stereotypes are sticky and take time to abate. But experience is an effective teacher and its lessons are not lost on those on the lookout for good employees. If group productivity really converges, then reliance on group generalizations should fade. It is ultimately in employers' interest to hire the most capable workers.

If skills deficits are the core problem, then what is the solution? Groups lagging behind must cultivate better job skills. Hard skills, including basic math, reading, writing, and analysis are first learned in school, and then enhanced later through specialized training. If basic skills are lacking, the temptation once again is to search for external policy fixes or programmatic interventions that can correct these deficits. Job training initiatives are often touted as the best approach. But such programs are famously expensive and ineffective. Despite significant public investment, they have not been shown to make much difference to labor market outcomes.[90] Rather, the evidence suggests that the foundations for good work skills are established in early childhood, well before formal schooling begins. Later interventions such as on-the-job training are too little too late. Once again, the argument is made that justice demands a massive effort. We are duty bound to provide whatever it takes to make up for early deficits and prepare everyone for good jobs. The problem, again, is that no known method can produce that result. A review of the evidence shows that even a "substantial increase in government-funded training services will not significantly improve the skills in the work force."[91] And even if training worked better, all groups would stand to gain, leaving racial disparities largely in place.[92] In sum, even large-scale job training efforts won't close race skill gaps.

What is true for education also holds for shortfalls on the job: A clear-minded consideration of the real nature of the problem requires a decisive shift away from grand programmatic interventions and institutional structures and toward individual initiative and what happens within families, neighborhoods, and communities. Existing disparities in job preparation are best addressed—indeed, ultimately can only be effectively addressed—by the persons and groups whose deficient performance leads to less desirable employment outcomes. As we have seen, what matters most are group customs, attitudes, and individual behaviors. This is not to say that structures of schooling, work, and compensation could not be rendered more fair generally, or that existing systems of taxation, benefits, and rewards among workers should remain undisturbed. But if the objective is to correct *racial* inequality, solutions do not lie in these directions.[93] The question at issue here is how, within the basic constraints of the current system, people from an underperforming group can come to achieve as much as others. The answers will not be found through manipulation by governments.

It may be objected that statistical discrimination generates "self-reinforcing disinvestment" by depriving blacks of a robust incentive to take steps to improve their employability. By practicing statistical discrimination, employers discount a particular person's credentials based on generalizations about the group. If managers will not give blacks' qualifications full weight, it is not "rational" for individual blacks to upgrade their skills and credentials or to strive to distinguish themselves from the average.[94]

This line of argument is faulty for several reasons. First, economists have recognized that there is no single "rational" response to statistical discrimination. Stereotyping is rarely all or nothing, and employers who give generalizations some credence do still pay attention to individuating characteristics. Persons who strive to distinguish themselves can still expect enhanced rewards, which will likely increase over time. Second, no one is destined to reduce his efforts by the prospect that his credentials will be discounted. A person has the choice to confront the somewhat harder struggle presented by stereotyping by working less hard or by working even harder to refute the generalizations. Although it is unfair to demand that people adopt the latter strategy, it may be necessary, at least as a transitional matter. More important, it is effective. There is reason to believe that groups that meet stereotyping with greater effort and greater self-development are the very ones who get ahead.[95] Certainly, there can be no argument that responding with *less* effort will produce that result. In any event, the contention here is that the only really enduring solution to lingering group generalizations is an upgrade in group qualifications across the board. The ultimate goal is to render stereotypes invalid once and for all.

Leaving aside the issue of how best to tackle rational discrimination, the most important point is that its prevalence should not be overstated. The evidence shows that racial discrimination, whether rational or irrational, is fading and is today a minor force in the operation of labor markets. Skill development is far more important, and performance does indeed pay off. Wage and employment data indicate that labor markets recognize and respond to perseverance and ability, and assign virtually equal rewards to workers with similar levels of skill. This provides reason to anticipate that if blacks could become as fully qualified as other groups, employment disparities would narrow significantly and eventually disappear.

Hard skills are only part of the story, however. Soft skills and other behavioral traits employers care about also affect job status and rewards. But soft skills are especially elusive. Dress, deportment, demeanor, speech patterns, helpfulness, friendliness, responsiveness, reliability, consistency, honesty, cooperativeness, alacrity, tenacity, thoroughness, and attention to detail may be manifest to employers on the front lines, but resist systematic study by social scientists or reliable documentation by watchdog observers. Although anecdotes abound,[96] there is little systematic data on racial differences in soft attributes.

Assuming group differences like these exist, the critical question is how to impart the necessary skills to those who possess too few. Conventional job training and educational programs do not usually address soft skills, and attempts to upgrade these attributes in adulthood have achieved only minimal success. Here the questions are similar and closely related to those that arise in the educational context. Habits of behavior have deep roots in home, neighborhood, and culture, and are most effectively taught early in life through observation, emulation, and family discipline. Although isolated programs that target adult socialization, such as *Strive*, have achieved some success in black inner-city neighborhoods, those results have yet to be generalized.[97] Not only are such programs necessarily limited in scope, but they are bound to be ineffective if subjects fail enthusiastically to embrace their objectives. Unfortunately, the enthusiasm is not always forthcoming. Some blacks seem ambivalent about such programs based on doubts about whether employers' behavioral expectations are legitimate, discriminatory, or an attempt to undermine cultural identity. Absent an all-out endorsement by community leaders and devoted, widespread participation by community members themselves, programs such as *Strive* are unlikely to have much impact.

In sum, the evidence suggests that racial parity in employment depends critically on behavioral reform, which is largely up to communities and individuals. The problem is not primarily rooted in broader external structures. Rather, it originates with norms that undermine the development of human capital, discourage prudent choices, and undermine socially optimal habits and behaviors. Changes in those norms must come from within.

Remedies for Family Disintegration

Finally, there is family. Well-functioning families are fundamental to individual and group success. Family structure is "the elephant in the room" of race. Without a dramatic turnaround in family life, blacks will have difficulty matching the success of other groups.

If family disintegration is a potent source of black disadvantage, what is the solution? Addressing this question requires understanding the demographics of family breakdown. Why marriage is so uncommon and out-of-wedlock childbearing so prevalent in the black community is not fully understood. Social scientists who have documented these patterns have struggled to explain them with only partial success. There is a growing consensus that racial differences in family formation and stability cannot be attributed to economic or material factors alone.[98] This consensus has important implications for how best to address the crisis of black families.

It is widely believed that a lack of marriageable men explains racial disparities in marriage rates and extramarital births. The root causes of an under-supply of potential husbands are in turn said to be mainly economic. Women want to marry men who are employed or employable and can command a good salary. Factors cited as contributing to black men's low marriageability include joblessness, low earnings, criminal activity, and incarceration. Using these measures, ratios of available men to women are indeed somewhat smaller for blacks than for Asians and whites. This is especially true for the best- and least-educated segments of the population. Among college-educated blacks, women significantly outnumber men, and poorly educated men are most likely to be unemployed or in jail.

Despite a relative shortage of desirable men, these ratios do not come close to explaining low marriage rates among blacks.[99] Demographers have concluded that racial differences in the availability of men conventionally deemed marriageable explain but a small portion of the steep decline in marriage rates among blacks during recent decades.[100] Significant numbers of employed black men now remain unmarried, and black men of every class are significantly less likely to marry than men with comparable education and earnings from other major racial and ethnic groups. Consistent with this observation, the recent decline in marriage among blacks cannot be explained by a general deterioration in the economic prospects of unskilled men. Although the income of college graduates has increased dramatically in recent years while men without a college degree have seen their salaries stagnate or decline, male high school graduates and dropouts do not earn significantly less than similarly educated men in past decades, when marriage rates were far higher for all ethnic groups, including blacks.[101]

In any event, marriage still carries important economic advantages, even for persons of modest skill, earning power, and economic prospects.[102] That well-functioning married couples can achieve greater economic well-being, regardless of social class, stands to reason. Marriage creates efficiencies and economies of scale and encourages sustained cooperation. In addition, there is evidence that marriage causes men to work harder and earn more.[103] In sum, contrary to common belief, economic factors and job prospects simply cannot explain family disintegration among blacks.[104]

Despite the absence of external obstacles to forming stable families and the clear economic advantages of married life, large numbers of black men and women choose not to marry.

Given the lack of obvious impediments to marriage, social scientists search for other explanations. Some have looked to the dynamics of marriage markets. Sarah McLanahan and Kristin Harknett have discovered that unmarried black couples who have recently had a child together marry at a lower rate than similar couples among other ethnic groups.[105] They also find a correlation between marriage rates among such couples and the number of same-race male marriage partners in the local geographic area.[106] Where the ratios are particularly favorable to black men, existing couples are least likely to marry. The authors speculate that men are reluctant to marry the mothers of their children in places where women outnumber men because there are more opportunities for men to "play the field."

Alternatively, recent ethnographic investigations suggest that sexual attitudes—including high mistrust between the sexes, lax views on early sexual activity and out-of-wedlock childbearing, and lack of commitment to monogamy and sexual fidelity—contribute to blacks' low marriage and high divorce rates.[107] Yet other research points to male behavior and women's response to it as impediments to the formation of stable relationships. In one ethnographic study, Kathryn Edin and Maria Kefalas interviewed a group of 162 single mothers in poor neighborhoods in Philadelphia—a group that included more than 50 blacks.[108] The authors claim that marriage is uncommon among this population because expectations for marriage have risen across the board. People now refuse to tie the knot unless they have first achieved economic success. But few unskilled men can make good on these aspirations because wages at the bottom have stagnated or declined. The authors' own findings, however, fail to support their account. Rather, their subjects' statements demonstrate that men's anti-social behavior, not unfulfilled economic expectations, are the main obstacle to matrimony among this group. The women did not complain of men's low earnings but of their financial profligacy, defiant attitudes, and lack of work discipline. Above all, the women objected to their men's flagrant sexual infidelity. Offspring by other partners—so-called "multiple partner fertility"—loomed especially large as barriers to stable and harmonious relationships. Although the authors' findings are not confined to the black community, multiple-partner fertility is especially prevalent in that group.[109] In sum, the attitudes and behaviors that discouraged these women from marrying are not obviously the outgrowth of material circumstances. Nor would they be alleviated by raising men's earnings or finding them better jobs.

Although well-meaning in their search for answers, these social-scientific attempts to identify ever more subtle "factors," causes, or explanations for observed patterns often reinforce the picture of subjects as the hapless and helpless victims of larger social forces. Even if some portion of nonmarriage and extramarital childbearing among blacks reflects a shortage in marriageable men, a focus on marriageability is potentially misleading in implying passivity toward conditions that make men less desirable mates. Many factors used by social scientists to gauge "eligibility"—such as earnings, employability, incarceration, law-breaking, drug dealing and use, and even early death—are not wholly or even largely exogenous. They depend crucially on individual conduct, including the very decisions to prepare for and commit to married life. Incarceration, joblessness, and low earnings do not just happen to people. Going to jail follows from the decision to break the law. Unemployment and low earnings most often result from poor planning, low effort, and inadequate attention to schooling or learning a trade. The commitment to marriage may itself raise earnings. Although higher-earning men are more likely to marry, that married men earn more is largely due to the *effects* of marital responsibility on earnings rather than to so-called selection, or the tendency of harder-working and higher-earning men to marry.[110] The decision to marry is in turn influenced by community norms and expectations.

Another explanation for lower marriage rates among blacks is that black women are more likely to work, which reduces the need for a mate. But black women's high workforce participation could as well represent women's self-protective *response* to men's unreliability and resistance to marriage. Other patterns impeding the formation of stable relationships, such as having children out-of-wedlock or by more than one partner, likewise stem from people's own behavioral choices—choices that reflect broader practices and attitudes toward marriage.

Finally, as already noted, Kristin Harknett and Sara McLanahan posit a connection between the background supply of marriageable men and the behavior of existing couples—even couples in which the man himself is employed. Because the supply of marriageable men is linked to their employment rate, the authors conclude, somewhat ambiguously, that "a shortage of employed [black] men explains a large portion of the racial and ethnic difference in marriage" among the couples in their study.[111] Elsewhere, they state that marriage market factors, including within-group male employment rates, help "determine" whether existing couples will marry.[112] These "explanations" have a strong mechanistic tone, implying a cause and effect relationship. The factors identified by the authors exert an "influence" that seems inescapable.

Once again, this rhetoric implies helplessness in the face of overwhelming social forces. That thinking is misguided. The authors are not looking at women who cannot find a man. The study's subjects are already part of a couple. The male partners are available and many are in a position to marry. Yet they decline to take on the obligations and constraints of matrimony. Thus, even if couples can somehow be viewed as "reacting" to the relative dearth of desirable male partners around them, it is a mistake to see these conditions as somehow "causing" people to reject marriage. Couples are not destined to respond in this way. Each couple's decision to avoid marriage represents a choice. Likewise, the surrounding supply of eligible men in turn reflects choices writ large. People remain free to change the underlying conditions or to alter their reactions.

The quality of the marriage market is itself a function of decisions—to become educated, to find a job, to refrain from breaking the law—that are ultimately within the power of individuals to make. Indeed, whether a man will make a good husband depends on factors that are largely within his own control. And even conceding that people are influenced or tempted by ambient circumstances, a marriage market favorable to men cannot plausibly be viewed as transforming the decision to marry into a hard struggle, let alone creating a brick wall. Favorable marriage markets do not function as obstacles, but rather as occasions to decide whether to commit, or not to commit, to a long-term relationship. But there is one choice that is always available: to marry the mother of one's child regardless of so-called market factors. Deciding to stay single and "play the field" after becoming a father may be understandable as an exercise in self-interest colored by strong cultural expectations. Although expedient in the short term, it is neither inevitable nor particularly admirable. And it is certainly not conducive to racial progress. The refusal of many black men to marry yields dysfunctional outcomes in the long term for present and future generations and the group as a whole.

It can be objected that norms are powerful in this arena. Collective practices and expectations exert an influence that individuals and couples cannot easily escape. Couples cannot resist being swayed; in some sense they cannot really "choose otherwise." But as Harknett and McLanahan's own data show, culture is not a monolith. Expectations surrounding marriage are not the same across groups, with patterns of response to marriage market conditions varying by race and ethnicity.[113] These variations, in turn, reflect different cultural norms.

This observation frames the central remedial question: How can dysfunctional norms surrounding marriage and reproduction be changed? Can they be transformed by outside interventions or pro-grams? The answer is almost certainly no. Although family structure is not completely resistant to policy influence—some have argued that decades of lax social welfare programs and family law reform have actually accelerated family decline[114]—the attitudinal shifts that would be necessary to revive the black nuclear family are not those that governments can readily bring about. In general, governments have so far proven more effective in undermining informal social in-stitutions than in strengthening those that have disintegrated. Thus, although external forces may have helped subvert the black family in recent years, family fragmentation cannot be reversed through any known program. Rather, strong families must be reconstructed from within. This fundamental point is easily forgotten in the never-ending quest for explanations and solutions.

To summarize, family structure and reproductive behavior are aspects of racial difference that are almost completely resistant to straightforward explanation and external control. The social science consensus is that material and economic conditions of the type that might be amenable to government intercession cannot fully explain existing patterns or account for more than a small part of class or race differences in family structure. The shape and character of fam-ily life are closely tied to decisions individuals make for themselves under the sway of informal expectations and understandings. No known policy can change these.

There is no top-down solution to the crisis in the black family.[115] All evidence suggests that recent developments are the result of dra-matic shifts in mores and norms of behavior. The government can-not fix these, and no social program has yet been devised that can arrest these trends. But that does not mean that the black family's decline is irreversible. As Roger Clegg points out in his review of a recent book by Tavis Smiley, a popular black talk show host, "This is the one problem that could be solved by the African-American community all by itself, without government help. It could go from 7 out of 10 [children born out of wedlock] to zero out of 10 in nine months, without passing a single bill or spending a dime."[116] Not only is this problem amenable to self-help, but self-correction is the only effective method for solving it. Internal reform cannot occur, however, until the problem is widely acknowledged, forcefully confronted, and understood as critical to equality. Family structure must move from the margins to the center of the black community's agenda. Fatherlessness, wholesale father abandonment, and free-wheeling "alternative families" should be rejected clearly, consistently, resoundingly, and without apology or hesitation. The nuclear, two-parent family should be embraced as the most desirable norm. The goal should be to emulate the strong, stable, cohesive structure of conventional families, which contribute so much to the success of other groups. All these moves are, at present, staunchly resisted. Tavis Smiley's treatment of the issue is emblematic. Although his 254-page book bills itself as a call for black self-help, it devotes "two sentences—and oblique ones at that"[117] to family structure and out-of-wedlock childbearing. Without more sustained attention, the needed reforms can hardly get off the ground.

The reluctance of many prominent blacks to confront the true magnitude of the problem or to acknowledge the central role of reproductive behavior in perpetuating group inequality is embedded in a broader cultural agenda. Those on the left, with whom blacks often make common cause, are committed to celebrating family diversity and to normalizing unconventional families. On their view, the two-parent, opposite-sex biological family is not inherently superior to other forms. Its relative success is a mere "construct"—a function of conventional structures that support its privileged status. These conventions should be replaced by new rules and programs. It is especially important not to stigmatize single mothers and non-traditional families, or to imply their lesser worth or status. Although some blacks may claim to reject these notions, this skepticism has not translated into action on the ground. The black family continues to deteriorate across the board.

Many social scientists and demographers now accept that group differences in family structure contribute to poverty and group inequality.[118] These differences have become more pronounced in the past few decades.[119] Although a veritable cottage industry has sprung up to analyze and respond to this development, the concern with family structure and its effects has not led to a clarion call for behavioral reform. Rather, the decline in marriage and the growth in fatherlessness are viewed as the product of adverse social conditions, or as the wages of governmental neglect, or as inevitable. Few within the policy community or the academy point to stronger and more functional families as an instrument for alleviating poverty. Nor is rebuilding the family seen as a first line strategy for achieving equality for disadvantaged groups.[120] Not surprisingly, exhortations to private action and self-directed reform are assigned the lowest priority or avoided entirely. Rather, alarm over family disintegration has yielded an endless stream of proposals for privately and publicly funded initiatives and interventions. If children from fatherless, broken, or single-parent families start out behind, then we must create and fund programs to enable them to catch up. The chief response remains to look to society to compensate for ill effects.

Although the impulse behind these efforts is worthy, and some programs may indeed ease the lot of discrete individuals, there is no reason to anticipate their making much difference to patterns of disadvantage overall. As already noted, all experience to date indicates that programmatic interventions can neither bring about fundamental changes in familial behavior nor make up for family breakdown. We don't know how to prevent domestic disorder; nor have we discovered how to reverse or compensate for its effects. This is not for lack of trying. Many programs to aid children from unstable families have been proposed, and many have been in place for years. Yet remedial idealism fuels the insistence that not enough has been done—that renewed efforts and a massive infusion of new resources are what is really needed. When it comes to aiding black families, endorsing ever more expensive and elaborate programs becomes the test of virtue; rejecting such programs, or doubting their effectiveness, defines bad faith. Yet, as with the injured pedestrian, there is no evidence that throwing money at the problem will work any real improvement.[121] Outside help has reached its limit, because the victim's contribution is now the rate-limiting step. Without a fundamental change in private lives, additional measures will prove ever more futile gestures with ever-diminishing returns.

Stable families—like adherence to traditional moral values, hard work, and obedience to law—are critical to success and prosperity in our society. Above all, they are crucial to equality among groups. Groups with orderly, cohesive families will always maintain a competitive edge, and those with weak families will always lag behind. Policies to strengthen families are at bottom ineffectual because the government is powerless to produce, or induce, prudent conduct in this arena. Well-functioning families cannot be conferred or bestowed. There is no effective blueprint for rescuing people from themselves. But that does not mean that family disintegration is inevitable. As with the injured pedestrian's recovery, the return to a healthy state is a project for victims. Only they can build strong families by committing to that goal and changing modes of living. Family structure and stability depend on cultural norms, personal resolve, and behavioral restraint. Reform must come from within individuals and communities.

Beyond School, Work, and Family

Some will object that racism and disparate treatment go far beyond the limited areas of education, employment, and family life already discussed. The claim is that racial discrimination abounds in many other sectors, including lending and consumer credit, housing, health care, policing, criminal justice, and law enforcement. Although a full review of these contentions cannot be undertaken here, some general points are in order.

In each case, careful scrutiny of the accumulated evidence reveals that the relative contribution of the type of biased treatment amenable to external correction is small as compared with the effects of behaviors and choices within the control of the target population. In general, observed disparities are best addressed not through public programs but through reform of the victim's own actions and strategies. Even where there is some evidence of discrimination amenable to external correction, its impact is, at most, minor and overwhelmed by other factors. In every case, effective solutions to observed problems mostly lie elsewhere. In these areas, as in others, race-based discrimination is a sideshow that distracts from more significant sources of disparate outcomes. Yet the temptation to devote disproportionate energy and attention to chasing down ever more elusive traces of bias is irresistible.

One accusation is that banks and credit card companies engage in "predatory lending" or other practices that work to the disadvantage of the poor or black consumers. The contention is that lenders tend to offer individuals from these groups less favorable terms. For example, some have claimed that auto dealers target the poor and minorities for more expensive loans or higher pricing. Ian Ayres has recently proposed that members of protected minority groups be allowed to sue auto dealers for loan charges in excess of competitive market rates.[122]

This proposal is ill-advised. Leaving aside the thorny problem of defining competitive market rates, the question comes down to why minority customers receive loans on less favorable terms. Although the evidence is conflicting, some data suggest that, even after controlling for financial position and higher default rates, the poor and minorities do sometimes pay more for cars and car loans. The reason, the argument goes, must be old-fashioned discrimination. However, excess charges in this market can be traced in significant part to consumers' failure to bargain and to search aggressively for better rates. To be sure, this does not rule out that dealers use group identity to generalize about customers and then to offer terms based on those generalizations. That is, dealers may perceive minorities, the poor, and women as less demanding, less price sensitive, and more concerned with other aspects of car purchases. To the extent dealers are "sensitive to [the] customer's responses" and accurately gauge those responses,[123] they are effectively engaging in "statistical discrimination" against some groups.[124]

If dealers' perceptions are correct, what is the best remedy for this situation? Whether and to what extent dealers' generalizations are accurate is difficult to verify. But the existence of group differentials in a vigorously competitive market for both loans and cars suggests that the problem might yield to consumer resistance and effort—in other words, to self-help. The expectation is that more aggressive bargaining and more knowledgeable shopping would eventually defeat the dominant generalizations and thereby reduce overcharging in the long run.

The problem with Ian Ayres's proposal is that it shelters car buyers from their own folly rather than prodding them to wise up. A well-functioning free market depends on savvy consumers. Legal rules that protect minorities from their own failure to comparison shop or bargain suspend reliance on this vital market role. Legal protections render low-income or minority consumers permanent wards of the state, requiring ongoing protection from other market actors. By removing incentives for unsophisticated consumers to inform themselves and exert their market power effectively, Ayres's proposal would undermine progress toward defeating the preconceptions and stereotypes that fuel price discrimination in the first place. There is much that targeted groups can do on this score, from providing education on consumer search to encouraging more aggressive bargaining to providing advice or independent channels for procuring low-cost credit. Exerting market power through self-help is, in the end, the only self-sustaining and long-term solution to the problem of lenders who seek to take advantage of consumers. These mechanisms of self-correction, in addition to yielding other financial benefits, are superior to regulation or litigation. They are certainly less cumbersome and expensive than oversight based on questionable economic theories and error-ridden administrative calculations.

Another commonplace accusation is that racism pervades the criminal justice system.[125] There is no question that blacks, and especially black men, are more likely than persons from other groups to be arrested and imprisoned for crimes.[126] But the critical question is whether this pattern reflects less-favorable treatment by police, prosecutors, and the courts, or whether blacks' disproportionate involvement with the criminal justice system reflects higher rates of criminal activity.

The most heated claims of bias surround the illegal drug trade, with controversy over whether blacks' high incarceration rates for drug offenses stem from greater involvement with drug dealing or from racially skewed patterns of criminalization and enforcement. The controversy is caught up with questions about the wisdom of the war on drugs that are beyond the scope of this book. Suffice it to say that, regardless of what society chooses to do about it, drug dealing is an important problem in the black community and one that is destructive of orderly lives and communities. Although ensuring fairness in drug-control efforts is an appropriate goal, drug dealing and usage are quintessential examples of problems that can only effectively be confronted from within. Without action by those directly involved, strenuous efforts to correct skewed law enforcement will have, at most, marginal effects.

As with disintegrating families and educational failure, so also with illegal drugs: To wait for others to solve the problem is to wait forever. The temptation is to demand rescue and to look to outsiders for solutions. But the government cannot prevent individuals from using illegal drugs. Although drug rehabilitation is much touted, such programs barely make a dent. Their effects pale in comparison with cultural norms surrounding drug trading and use. It does not help that the rhetoric among students of the problem is overwhelmingly fatalistic, with inner city drug dealing viewed as the expected by-product of pervasive racism and deprivation. The call, once again, is for more programs to control drugs, provide alternatives to the drug trade, and rehabilitate drug users. But such efforts will surely fail. There is no reason to believe that costly reforms will work a fundamental change in high rates of drug dealing and use within the black community.

For non-drug crimes, the picture is much clearer. Contrary to frequently voiced accusations and despite a voluminous literature intent upon demonstrating discrimination at every turn, there is almost no reliable evidence of racial bias in the criminal justice system's handling of ordinary violent and non-violent offenses. Rather, the facts overwhelmingly show that blacks go to prison more often because blacks commit more crimes. As a noted criminal law scholar sympathetic to black concerns stated in an exhaustive summary of the literature, "[v]irtually every sophisticated review of social science evidence on criminal justice decision making has concluded, overall, that the apparent influence of the offender's race on official decisions concerning individual defendants is slight."[127] With respect to arrests, "few or no reliable, systematic data are available that demonstrate systematic discrimination." Rather, "arrests can by and large be taken as reasonable reflections of the involvement in serious crime of members of different racial groups."[128] Likewise, and despite the widely held belief to the contrary, blacks are not singled out for stricter or more frequent prosecution. Nor do they receive longer sentences once criminal history and other sentencing factors are taken into account. In short, for ordinary violent and property crimes, "the answer to the question, 'Is racial bias in the criminal justice system the principal reason that proportionately so many more blacks than whites are in prison,' is no."[129]

In this vein, consider a 2000 report indicating that black youths receive harsher treatment for offenses throughout the juvenile justice system, as reflected, for example, in higher rates of assignment to detention centers and out-of-home supervision.[130] As one lead researcher on the report admits,[131] the study made no attempt to investigate the reasons for these disparities. Specifically, it did not control for factors, such as a youth's family situation and social supports, that influence the need for institutional placement. But the strength and stability of families and the character of neighborhoods to which juvenile offenders return undeniably affect how much control will be exerted over them and how much supervision they need and will receive. These in turn bear on the risks of recidivism, the danger to the public from future lawbreaking, and the potential for reform. Demographic data suggest that black youth are more likely to come from an unstable home situation, which would tend to enhance the risk that black juvenile offenders will repeat their unlawful conduct.[132] Claims of irrationality or animus cannot be substantiated without taking into account such background differences that are relevant to official placement decisions and outcomes.

Commentators nonetheless repeatedly stress the deleterious effects on the black community of the high rates of conviction and imprisonment of black men.[133] The objection that too many blacks are in jail gives rise to the question of what should be done about it. Should those convicted of crimes receive lighter sentences or just go free? These alternatives ignore the fact that violent crimes committed by blacks most often victimize other blacks. Easing criminal enforcement against black men does not help, and indeed could well hurt, these potential victims.[134] More importantly, the debate over incarceration rates distracts from the most effective and enduring solution to crime, which is for individuals to commit fewer of them. Once again, this step lies within the power of the very persons who complain of ill treatment. But that isn't the way many students of the problem see it. Their outlook is fatalistic, committed to a mechanistic model of social causation, and fixated on external relief. The oft-repeated claims are that incarceration does more harm than good, that going easier on criminals makes things better by restoring men to their families and communities,[135] and that in any event the conditions of black life are inevitably "criminogenic."

It is society's duty, through government, to change that. It follows that society, and only society, can do so.

With crime, as with fragile families, drugs, joblessness, and underachievement, the habit persists of regarding obstacles as insurmountable and of looking to others to remove them. But high crime rates in the black community are far from inevitable. The first step to enduring improvement is to stop looking outward and to regard internal reform as the only workable strategy. As with the injured pedestrian, the victim must cure himself.

CHAPTER 4

The Psychology of Victimization

The discussion in the previous chapter supports the generalization that most black-white disparities can now be traced to blacks' lower qualifications on neutral criteria or to simple differences in behavior. Ongoing race-based discrimination—whether conscious or unconscious, rational or irrational—explains a very small part of existing differences in educational attainment, jobs, wages, family structure, consumer credit rates, and involvement with the criminal justice system. Similar data are available on health, home ownership, housing, and other indicators of social well-being. These observations counsel a decisive shift in emphasis away from government programs and broad structural changes toward an inner focus on reforming the culture and altering individual values and behaviors.

It may be argued that there is no need to make a choice between the two. Why not pursue strategies on both fronts? The black community should advocate self-help while also vigorously pushing for government assistance and political change. Instances of this dual approach abound. During his presidential campaign, then Senator (now President) Barack Obama told a predominantly black inner city audience in Chicago that government help "will not make any difference unless we have a change of heart." He nonetheless promised to "keep fighting in Washington for more money and more programs."[1] Likewise, in *Race Matters,* Cornel West advocates a "politics of conversion." Blacks must turn away from nihilism and self-destructive behavior and toward a "love ethic." But he also attributes the "shattering of black civil society" to "structural conditions that shape the suffering and lives of people." He warns that "advocates of a politics of conversion" should "never lose sight" of "the poor black situation," which can only be addressed through a political agenda.[2]

Although this dual approach is superficially appealing, it has outlived its usefulness. After decades of improvement, progress has stalled and the situation for blacks has deteriorated on a number of fronts. In the face of persisting disparities, the temptation to see white racism as the defining burden and the decisive barrier remains irresistible. Invoking ongoing discrimination as the first and best explanation for existing gaps remains the litmus test for dedication to the cause of racial equality. But this position has now become a potent engine of misplaced priorities. The continuing obsession with rooting out racism means that a growing amount of effort is directed at an ever-diminishing part of the problem. Likewise, invoking the amorphous category of "structural discrimination" encourages passivity by directing attention to what others can do and what money can buy. The objectionable "structures" too often come down to conditions that blacks themselves have allowed to persist but could in fact correct. Indeed, in most instances, blacks are now the only ones who *can* correct them. Political solutions to these problems can only go so far, and go less far today than ever before.

With so many forces arrayed against a realistic assessment of the dilemma, priorities will inevitably be skewed. The gross imbalance in effort and psychic investment is not without cost. Measures designed to reduce discrimination and "structural racism" will have very little long-term payoff in the current climate. Attention and resources are not unlimited, so any efforts expended in this direction will be unavailable for other priorities. Devoting energy to fighting discrimination and procuring outside assistance will inevitably slight the paramount imperative, which is to turn away from external solutions towards reform from within.

The distortion in emphasis has a potential psychological dimension. Not only is the fight against racism now disproportionate to its actual real-world impact, but the obsession with external injuries and remedies has become a distraction and a drain. Is it possible to pursue an arduous program of self-improvement while simultaneously thinking of oneself as a victim of grievous mistreatment and of one's shortcomings as a product of external forces? As a practical matter, it may be difficult to operate effectively on two tracks. Seeing the surrounding society as alien and hostile promotes an oppositional attitude that undermines the will to succeed. But it also generates a passivity that extends to victims' expectations. Once again, the rescue fantasy rears its head. It's all too easy to wait for others to act and to look to others for solutions. Maintaining the outlook needed for self-criticism and self-improvement may be fundamentally incompatible with directing one's energies toward securing outside help. Focusing on the actions of others may sap the determination necessary to achieve difficult internal changes. Deemphasizing or abandoning the elusive quest for racial justice may in fact be a precondition for real progress.

Is the sense of oneself as a victim psychologically debilitating? That self-concept comes into play in too many contexts to allow easy generalization. For blacks, victimization has been a defining part of group identity throughout our national history. The image of blacks as psychically damaged by their oppressive treatment and lowly social position is longstanding and has too often been misused to argue for inferiority.[3] That such a self-concept does more harm than good cannot easily be demonstrated and remains speculative in the context of race. But that does not mean that a psychological perspective on racial disparities has nothing to contribute to an understanding of the current dilemma.

Work in social psychology provides insights into the personal attributes most conducive to positive life outcomes. Such studies reveal
that individuals differ in their attitudes towards the roots of success
and failure. A person with an "external locus of control" tends to believe that his destiny is largely out of his hands. The most important
forces in his life are bad luck or social impediments such as discrimination. In contrast, someone with an "internal locus of control" regards his fate as largely a product of his own actions, decisions, and
choices.[4] Such a person ignores or discounts external barriers. He
believes he can improve his life by dint of his own efforts.

There is empirical evidence that an internal locus of control is
associated with positive outcomes, including higher educational
achievement and greater job success.[5] Internal locus, for example,
predicts high math scores and other forms of academic attainment
for students from diverse backgrounds.[6] There is also some evidence that blacks tend to have a more external locus of control than
whites.[7] Studies conducted in the 1960s found that black children
were more externally oriented than whites,[8] that external control
expectancies among prison inmates were significantly higher for
blacks than for whites,[9] and that blacks and whites differed on average in self-concept.[10] Later research suggested that a diminished
sense of internal agency in blacks is associated with "system-blame,"
or the habit of attributing failure to an unjust system that impedes
individual progress.[11] Differences in these measures are linked to
performance. One recent study has shown that internal locus of
control is highly correlated with adult earnings and completed education in black men.[12] Another older study found that although
black and white students were similar in embracing the abstract notion that people are generally in control of their lives, fewer blacks
held the concrete, personalized belief that they could exert control
over their own existence.[13] The same study also found that, whereas
both abstract and concrete internal loci of control were positively
correlated with academic achievement, concrete locus of control
was much more predictive of educational outcomes.[14]

Although suggestive, the literature on locus of control counsels caution. First, many studies date from the 1960s and 1970s, when race discrimination was more pervasive.[15] Although recent research suggests that racial disparities in self-concept still persist, more extensive investigation of the connection between attitudes and outcomes is in order. Second, although internal locus of control has been linked to desirable behaviors, the literature on race is spotty, and some studies are equivocal.[16] Third, correlation is not causation. Blaming others may promote failure, but persons more likely to fail may also tend to "self-handicap," or rationalize their failures, by pointing to external obstacles.[17] Nonetheless, the data suggesting racial differences in external locus of control do raise the possibility that attributing racial disparities to outside forces like discrimination may foster passivity and underachievement. By providing a ready excuse for falling short, conceiving of oneself as a victim may operate as a drain rather than a strength.

Can blacks really give up on seeing themselves as victims? The truth is that blacks have been victimized by white racism, and this treatment is the cause of many present ills. But acknowledging these truths poses a dilemma. Although recognizing that others have inflicted injury is consistent with regarding self-help as the only workable route to repair, victims will not find that understanding easy to embrace. As the parable of the pedestrian illustrates, what makes sense in theory can be difficult to accept in practice. The self-help insight meets resistance because it offends our deepest sense of justice. And acting on it calls for enormous effort. Constantly reminding oneself of the wrongs committed by others may sap the will needed to address the consequences of these wrongs. And the injuries inflicted undermine the ability to do so.

Yet the experience of other groups shows that recognizing past insults while relying on oneself to mitigate them is not psychologically impossible. Jewish mindfulness of historical persecution, for instance, has neither hobbled the group's social and economic progress nor significantly compromised individual Jews' sense of control over day-to-day failures and successes. Persons who are victimized by other types of conduct confront similar issues. It is a staple of therapy for early psychological trauma, such as childhood physical or sexual abuse, that victims must restore themselves to psychological health. Many therapists accept that "learning self-care" is indispensable to recovery from traumatic stress. That task, by its nature, is arduous. "The concept of self-care for adult survivors of childhood abuse is an inherent paradox" because abuse weakens the ability to engage in self-healing.[18] Yet some victims do manage, through great effort, to restore their sense of well-being and live normal lives.

In the struggle to commit to self-renewal, the broader culture offers blacks diminishing help. The old discourse of individual character, moral freedom, cultivated virtue, and personal responsibility is no longer in fashion. Discussions of race have been hijacked by variations on sociological thinking that are favored by professional academics and widely expressed in popular culture. In the words of David Brooks, an "environmental, sociological explanation of events" has replaced "the language of morality and character."[19] In seeing hardships as the product of broad structures and behavior as the outgrowth of determining conditions, this view promotes a passive sense of self as a plaything of outside forces and a casualty in the epic clash of group interests. By drawing down cultural capital accumulated in past eras, some groups escape the effects of this fatalistic outlook. But for the most vulnerable, including those whose past history already fosters a sense of helplessness, this approach can be counterproductive and even crippling. The supreme irony is that those who have the longest way to go will be most severely affected. At the present juncture, when opportunities for advancement have never been greater, a strong sense of agency is far more adaptive than an obsession with social causation. Yet sociological thinking has never been more dominant or more effective in undermining progress.

CHAPTER 5

Is Self-Help Possible?

Self-help is an abstraction. Even if alternatives are futile, it does not follow that self-correction represents a viable means of achieving racial equality. Although self-help may be necessary, what is the likelihood that recommended reforms will occur? Can we really expect the victim to help himself? Spontaneous and self-directed behavioral change must prove itself in practice. It must be a real possibility and not just a good idea.

Because individuals operate within groups, the feasibility of internal reform cannot be assessed without considering the role of group culture. The critical context for the proposed behavioral changes is the cultural community, which exerts a strong pull on individual choices. This is especially true for blacks, who tend to be socially isolated from other groups. Indeed, group norms represent the "external force" that matters most to how individual blacks respond to the conditions they presently face. The course proposed here is thus intimately connected to an understanding of cultural influence and the possibility of cultural change.

Group norms, once entrenched, are tenacious. Altering established behaviors poses a challenge of coordinating collective action because group patterns can frustrate individual efforts or make it harder to succeed. The power of norms is often a matter of the numbers. It's difficult to avoid or reject dysfunctional behaviors if many of one's social contacts exemplify them. Ostracizing felons becomes harder as more men do time in jail. Single motherhood loses its stigma if many mothers lack a husband. A faithful husband is a chump if many others play the field. A devoted father looks the fool if other fathers worry mostly about themselves. And studying hard seems abnormal or even defiant if most of one's friends don't care about school.

Moreover, many cultural practices are interactive. Family formation is especially thorny in this regard. A stable marriage norm requires a high degree of coordination. Men and women must be willing to make and to honor similar choices. They must routinely adopt a range of virtuous behaviors relating to work, sexual restraint, finances, and mutual cooperation that make them attractive partners and that promote domestic harmony. Robust norms also depend on critical mass. As more couples adhere to salutary patterns, it becomes easier for others to do the same. This means that the people who pioneer reforms face the hardest (and loneliest) struggle. Finally, some norms, such as contempt for academic achievement as a form of "acting white," are caught up with group identity.[1] Those who defy them can be viewed as turning their backs on friends, or as "selling out."[2] Indeed, the costs of being out of step with maladaptive patterns are among the most serious impediments confronting individuals within the black community today.

In light of these obstacles, is cultural reform realistic? Grappling with this is a tall order because cultural dynamics are still poorly understood. Work on group norms is in its infancy, and social science is far from achieving a full understanding of how cultural values arise, let alone how to alter them.[3] Little is known about the conditions that foster evolution from within. Nonetheless, social science is not wholly devoid of ideas for approaching these complexities.

Concepts of group dynamics such as "contagion" or "tipping" have entered the lexicon and helped inform our understanding of how patterns of conduct might evolve over time.[4] Game-theory models of group interaction also hold promise by showing how dysfunctional customs can take hold. As economist Robert Frank has noted, practices can arise that benefit individuals (at least in the short term) but harm the community—that are good for one and bad for all. Game theory also sheds light on the vital function of morality: Frank and others have observed that moral rules help coordinate socially cooperative strategies that foster group success. Some social scientists have developed models of adherence to group customs as a way to signal group identity and enhance solidarity.[5] It is hoped that these insights will eventually help shed light on the best methods for modifying norms and creating more constructive patterns of social life.

Recent reversals in social convention, such as the growth of a strong taboo against smoking, show that norms are not fixed. But such examples have failed to yield generalized models that can be applied to the tangle of conventions that perpetuate group disadvantage. Cultures consist of "a million small habits, expectations, [and] tacit understandings about how people should act and map out their lives."[6] In light of this complexity, it is not surprising that decades of social science research have produced no workable methods for moving entrenched patterns of work, family, and educational achievement in more desirable directions.

It may be objected that government programs are not entirely powerless to alter personal behavior. Indeed, conservative critics claim that programs like Aid for Families with Dependent Children have discouraged self-reliance, hard work, and family solidarity.[7] But it doesn't follow that government action can reverse these effects. Beneficial habits depend on a delicate ecology of coordination and restraint. The government's ability to erode the culture need not be matched by its ability to effect a reconstruction. Unfortunately, no tried and true blueprint for cultural renewal yet exists, and no effective protocol has yet been devised.

Black cultural reform is, if anything, an even more formidable project. Remedial idealism provides a potent source of resistance and generates widespread confusion surrounding what justice requires. In addition, social science has not definitively established which social arrangements and behaviors best promote success. But, finally, the most important challenge is internal and political. The problem ultimately comes down to one of collective action. A way must be found to coordinate behavior. The most critical tasks, therefore, are to achieve consensus and to act on it. But just as there is no surefire solution to racial inequality through public policy, so there is also no ready formula for reaching agreement on what changes are needed and for orchestrating these changes from within.

Nonetheless, it is possible to say something about the form self-renewal efforts will take. A dramatic transformation in the attitude of black leadership is indispensable. And small, homegrown organizations within the black community are sure to play a crucial role. Although efforts of this type already exist, they would need to proliferate dramatically, grow decisively in power and influence, and profoundly reorient their focus and rhetoric.[8]

Important ideological and political forces impede movement in this direction. Those with vested interests in special assistance for black Americans will not readily give up their influence. Black leaders are understandably reluctant to relinquish the model of political grievance inherited from the postwar civil rights era. This model has brought blacks power, access, money, and patronage in a range of public and private institutions.[9] And black politicians are poorly situated to lead the black community in the proposed direction. Politicians are in the business of enacting programs and securing resources for their constituencies, and black politicians have long been committed to these goals. Advocating an inward turn towards private action does not sit easily with this role.

Specific objectives that are essential to black progress are also likely to meet resistance. Reversing family disintegration, strengthening marriage, and restoring the dominance of the conventional two-parent family are surely essential to closing racial gaps over the long term. But as already noted, these goals run contrary to received ideas and a formidable array of social trends. Elite opinion holds that single parenthood is a viable, even laudable, family model that, with proper public support, can work as well as the traditional nuclear family.[10] The general public increasingly embraces family diversity, abhors stigma, and is loath to pass judgment on sexual and reproductive choice.[11] Feminists disparage the notion that large numbers of unattached men can be destructive of communities, or that enlisting men in nurturing the next generation is essential to a civilized existence. Black leaders are reluctant openly to criticize out-of-wedlock childbearing because single parenthood is so commonplace within the community.[12]

Asking the black family to return to more conventional forms is asking a lot. Single parenthood and extramarital childbearing are increasing rapidly for most demographic groups. Only among Asians and well-educated whites are non-traditional families still rare.[13] How, then, can blacks reasonably be expected to resist these powerful trends? That the task is truly heroic does not change the fundamental reality: Blacks will not catch up with other groups unless their families achieve greater order and cohesion. If future generations are to close the gap in human capital, the black family must arrest its decline.

If more intact families are the goal, then how can that goal be realized? Conventional policy instruments have proven utterly ineffective. There is no alternative to internal reform. And, apart from the futility of government action in this arena, rebuilding the family is a task radically unsuited to official intervention. As a matter of law and politics, government actors are bound to an evenhanded "value neutrality" that undermines vigorous advocacy and impedes effective action. Government officials cannot tout the superiority of marriage with the robust partiality available to private leaders. Anti-discrimination and equality norms block many official efforts to favor married couples in law and policy.[14] Yet, without aggressive and concrete steps that effectively "discriminate" against less functional types of families, it is hard to see how government can discourage informal unions and extramarital reproduction. In addition, government can do little to socialize men and women to the restraints and demands of sustained marital commitment. Although some have advocated government-sponsored media campaigns to change cultural attitudes toward sexuality and childbearing, the limits placed on what governments can say means these public pronouncements can never work as well as private initiatives. Those initiatives must begin with the community.

What is to be done? Although offering nothing like a complete program, the list below suggests prerequisites for any constructive reform. The first steps are to clear up confusion and banish the standard rhetorical moves and objections. Without new ways of thinking, no decisive change can occur.

1. Separate Liability and Remedy

Recognize the distinction between liability and remedy, between how the present dilemma came about and how to fix it. Reject remedial idealism and embrace remedial realism. Remember that those who inflict an injury cannot necessarily repair it and that the victim may have no choice but to take charge of his own recovery. In the case of race, accept the parable of the injured pedestrian. Acknowledge a key role for the victim's choices, decisions, and behaviors in perpetuating disadvantage. Accept that outsiders and the government can never bring about racial equality. Admit that, although others are responsible for the present dilemma and society as a whole must do all it can to address it, those efforts have reached the point of limited usefulness. The victim's input is now the rate-limiting step. Key reforms must come from within individuals and the community.

2. Accept That Justice May Not Be Achievable

This approach cautions that racial justice may never be attained. Is it fair to charge blacks with the weighty task of self-improvement when others' wrongs have made their burden so great? The answer is no. But that doesn't change reality. Just as the careless driver can bankroll recovery but cannot make the pedestrian walk again, the government and society can supply resources and create opportunities but cannot return blacks to their rightful place. Try as they might, they cannot fully restore the victims' capacities. Only the victim can do that. Because this insight runs contrary to fundamental principles of justice, it meets stiff resistance. Like the injured pedestrian, those who have suffered the harms from wrongdoing insist that they should not have to bear the costs of recovery. Maintaining a sharp separation between causes and cures is essential to relinquishing this view and accepting the inevitable burden.

3. Avoid the Trap of Sociological Thinking

The proposition that the key to closing racial gaps is not more resources or programs but the victim's self-help rests on a particular approach to human conduct. All individuals, including black victims of historic oppression, have a choice about whether and how to respond to circumstances that demand a hard struggle. They maintain the ability to reason and understand. They are capable of reflection and self-motivated change. These tenets sit uneasily with an analytic, social-scientific view of human behavior. As noted, social science tends toward a reductionist model of social causation that views external, structural factors as determining and ultimately limiting human choice. This approach cannot be definitively refuted. It can be countered only by an alternative perspective grounded in basic human experience. That perspective maintains a clear distinction between the current impediments to racial progress and the hard and fast obstacles of the past. It takes freedom and agency seriously and embraces the possibility of self-motivated change. It credits the potential for a spontaneous "conversion experience" whereby people discard old illusions, find a new path, and redirect their lives.

In a society that provides reasonable opportunities for self-betterment, hard struggles are fundamentally different from brick walls. Although behavioral patterns are tenacious, they are not irrevocable. Upbringing, family, life experiences, and cultural assumptions shape attitudes, beliefs, and values. Countering these forces is sometimes arduous and costly. But the obstacles are not insurmountable: Real choices are still possible. People do in fact respond differently to similar constraints. The same possibilities apply for culture. Like the decision at the individual level to take a different life path, the decision to alter group practices is not wholly foreclosed. Although cultural evolution is rendered more difficult by the need to coordinate and cooperate, the constructive evolution of communities ultimately rests on human determination and choice. In this realm, inner-directed change must always be regarded as a real possibility.

4. Shift the Focus from Structure to Culture

The remedial approach counsels a more serious and clear-eyed focus on culture, psychology, and the internal dynamics of group behaviors. Emphasis on vaguely defined structures and the material aspects of institutional arrangements should give way to a renewed interest in how the family and group can shape attitudes, outlook, expectations, and individual choice. The goal should be to promote psychological habits and character traits that foster a law-abiding, constructive, and self-sufficient life. Achieving this requires understanding how group dynamics can impede individual efforts to break out of maladaptive patterns. It also requires accepting the collective nature of solutions.

Perhaps the most critical insight that emerges from an appreciation of the role of group dynamics is the need to develop a consensus on self-help. There must be widespread agreement that, in most key respects, what persons within the community do for themselves matters more than what outsiders can do for them. The need for change must be recognized broadly, and the commitment to make changes must become widely shared. In addition, the importance of group dynamics must be more openly acknowledged. How some people behave is not just their own business. The conduct of others within the group is the most important "structure" constraining whether individuals can break out of old patterns and better their lives.

Achieving these objectives requires moral clarity and judgment. Community leaders must be willing to define standards and values in the areas of family, education, and other aspects of personal conduct and community life, even in defiance of the way most people live. Above all, they should repudiate the idea that achieving these goals must await improved conditions, new programs, more funding, or institutional reforms.

But the real challenge is moving from aspiration to conduct. Above all, cultural change proceeds from an understanding that numbers matter: How *most* people actually think and behave sets expectations more effectively than mere rhetoric. Real progress requires achieving a critical mass of people living up to worthy norms. Concrete goals should include turning around some key ratios. Instead of two-thirds of black children born out of wedlock, the objective should be to reduce this to one-third within a generation. Instead of most black men and women failing to get married, marriage must be the choice for the great majority. Instead of most black children failing to read at their grade level or higher, the goal should be that most will achieve this degree of proficiency within a decade. Instead of too often serving as havens of danger, menace, and crime, minority neighborhoods should strive to make themselves models of safety, decorum, and civic order.

There is no ready formula for bringing these changes about. But they will not occur without people working together to alter the conditions of their lives. The goal is to develop "collective efficacy"—the capacity of community members to improve outcomes on the basis of shared expectations.[15] Although it is commonplace to stress "external structures," this rhetoric distracts from the fundamental insight: Collective efficacy is not a goal that can be engineered from without.

5. Change the Rhetoric

Words matter. Discussions of race are too often couched in euphemistic language that implies the play of irresistible, morally neutral, disembodied forces. Those who address black men's anti-social behavior speak of the "plight" of black men. Criminal activity is referred to as "the problem of crime." Students' misbehavior, academic indifference, and lack of effort are denominated as "school failure" or "poor schools." And the decision to bear children out of wedlock is called "family disintegration." Substituting nouns for verbs removes the victim as active agent. The implication is that terrible things are happening, not that people are making them happen. Employing the language of action and choice rather than the rhetoric of conditions shifts the focus to the power of victims themselves.[16]

6. Criticize Failure and Emulate Success

The current climate is not one in which cultural self-criticism can flourish. Racial pride militates against internal cultural scrutiny, and fear of loss of cultural identity inhibits calls to relinquish common group practices. Existing patterns, however dysfunctional, are rationalized as the understandable response to oppressive outside forces. Indeed, there is a general social taboo against labelling customs common to a disadvantaged group maladaptive. But blacks should resist the impulse to circle the wagons. Fatherlessness and single parenthood are not worth defending. Educational underachievement is not worth keeping. Law-breaking and defiance of legitimate authority can never be a source of enduring pride. These patterns do not express identity, establish diversity, or represent an "alternative" lifestyle choice. Rather, they stand in the way of achieving group progress.

One key impediment is black leaders' lack of a consistent stance towards bourgeois values. While some wholeheartedly embrace them, others imply they are arbitrarily imposed, culturally biased, unworkable, futile, or unreasonable under presently oppressive conditions.[17] Likewise, cultural products like rap and hip-hop music, which often extol violence and misogyny, are sometimes strongly condemned but are held by others as vital expressions of an "authentically black" experience.[18] This mixed message, although hard to avoid, is confusing and counterproductive. Just as no group has progressed in America without maintaining strong families, so no group can succeed without wholeheartedly embracing respect for law, enterprise, persistence, thrift, prudence, restraint, sobriety, and hard work. Ambivalence about these core values undermines the cause of equality.

Yet another important obstacle to cultural self-renewal is a taboo against the studied emulation of other cultures. Mainstream discourse shies away from drawing contrasts among group characteristics that bear on social outcomes.[19] Still, comparisons are not entirely banished from the scene, with some conservative writers forthrightly addressing behavioral and cultural roots of group success.[20] In addition, social scientists interested in the determinants of school and intellectual achievement have investigated group differences, attributing disparities among Asian, white, and black students to attitudes towards education[21] and childrearing practices.[22] Some studies allude to perceptions about work ethic and work-related conduct that lead employers to favor recent immigrants over native-born minority workers.[23]

The sources of racial and ethnic differentials are worthy of study by groups seeking to better themselves. Yet the obstacles to this are many. Holding some groups up as examples to others risks wounding the fragile pride of the less-favored. Such comparisons also fly in the face of the conventional wisdom of "diversity," which is that all cultural identities are equally valid, worthy, and good. Comparing blacks with others is often dismissed as omitting the explanatory trump card: the unique fact of anti-black racism. Finally, unflattering comparisons raise the specter of biological differences. The contribution of genes and environment to differential group outcomes is sensitive and difficult to sort out.[24] Yet an understanding of the nature of observed disparities is needed to develop effective internal strategies for addressing racial inequality.

7. Resist Open-Ended Demands for Help

According to the remedial ideal, justice requires that the wrongdoer fix what is broken. If white society caused racial inequality, the government and society must eliminate it. This simple imperative fuels the moralistic fallacy and engenders a powerful rescue fantasy. If society must undo the harms it has inflicted, it follows that society can do so. If the wrongdoer in the form of white society or the government has not yet brought about racial equality, then by definition not enough has been done. That efforts to date have not worked proves only that existing remedial measures are inadequate. We simply must do more to reverse the legacy of racism.

This logic drives a demand for ever more strenuous efforts and fuels a perpetual search for programmatic solutions. Some combination of public policies and outside initiatives—some as yet undiscovered manipulations—will achieve racial justice. Policy analysts and social scientists must redouble their efforts to identify measures that will reverse the corrosive effects of discrimination. All forms of bias, however elusive, must be aggressively uncovered and rooted out. We must devise ever more elaborate schemes of social engineering, and politicians must muster the resources and political will to put such programs in place. If success continues to elude us, that just means we have not yet hit on the right formula. We must keep searching until we find the solution. We must not stop until we discover how to push the right knobs and turn the right dials. Then racial gaps will close.

This is a recipe for limitless grievance. Because the wrongdoer's efforts can never work a complete cure or even make much progress, there can be no end to demands. Remedial closure cannot be achieved and the quest for recompense never ends. The victim remains forever unsatisfied. The parable of the pedestrian shows the way out. The remedial ideal cannot always be attained. At some point, the pedestrian's condition will no longer yield to the driver's help. Additional assistance delivers diminishing returns and, ultimately, futility. Likewise, the persistence of group disadvantage does not mean society has failed to do enough. That efforts to date have not worked does not mean those efforts are inadequate. Yet concerns about futility and efficacy are often forgotten in the urgent insistence that justice be done. Unquestioning enthusiasm for new programs and initiatives becomes the true test of moral virtue, and opposition or doubts about their effectiveness define bad faith. Advocating self-help meets staunch and outraged resistance, is equated with callous indifference, and invites opprobrium.

This discourse breeds resentment and polarization. Those who are eager for racial progress but skeptical of programmatic initiatives know their views are regarded with disdain. Those who believe that doing something is better than doing nothing feel disappointed and betrayed when their well-meaning (and expensive) efforts yield minimal or nonexistent results. The search for culprits never ends, with veiled or overt accusations of racism the last refuge of dashed hopes. The parable of the pedestrian shows the path out of this impasse. Turning away from external fixes is not racism and does not deny responsibility. It only acknowledges the present reality, which is that achieving full equality is now up to the victims.

8. Stop Operating on Two Tracks

Self-help has long been an important idea in the black community, albeit one easily dismissed and often denigrated. But calls for internal reform are almost always coupled with demands for government programs. The mixed message has not worked. Although the temptation to look to government is overwhelming, blacks should resist. Appeals to external assistance drain energy and divert attention. The continued faith in rescue through policy impedes the psychological shift necessary to make self-help truly effective. Accepting that outsiders will not solve the problem calls for an entirely new mentality that turns decisively away from past aspirations. It requires seeing that the most effective action is not politics as usual but of another order entirely—that the greatest need at present is not for a more vigorous attack on racism, or more help, or new programs, but for a conversion experience, a change of heart, a novel direction, and a dramatic new movement. Above all, a drastic reorientation in thinking is necessary. The victim must realize that, although others have wronged him, his fate is in his own hands. Through the exercise of reason and understanding, he can make different and better choices. Energy expended on politics impedes these realizations.

Giving up on political solutions does not mean abandoning all organized efforts to improve life within the black community. Far from it. Rather, it means turning away from imposed, bureaucratic approaches in favor of private, small scale, homegrown initiatives that stress the importance of mundane practice, mutual support, and individual enterprise. Such initiatives now exist in the black community.[25] Money or advice from outsiders can help support these efforts but can never substitute for them. The impetus must come from within.

9. Resist Double Standards

The U.S. Department of Justice recently filed suit against New York City to challenge the entrance exam for municipal firefighters, which blacks and Hispanic candidates fail at a much higher rate than whites.[26] The lawsuit is based on the doctrine of "disparate impact," which originates in the Supreme Court's decision in *Griggs v. Duke Power Company.*[27] In that case, the Court held that a racially neutral hiring standard (a high school diploma requirement) that screened out more black than white applicants for custodial jobs violated federal civil rights laws unless the employer could demonstrate a link between that requirement and job performance.

Disparate impact claims may be useful in some cases, as when hiring is based on immutable features (such as height, weight, or appearance) that disadvantage one race or sex, or when job standards threaten cherished values (such as religious beliefs). When disparate impact suits challenge standards or qualifications that bear on the development of human capital, however, they threaten to become counterproductive. The qualifying test at issue in the New York lawsuit assessed basic reading, reasoning, and knowledge relevant to the firefighters' job.[28] Attacking the test sends the message that blacks cannot learn or develop the skills the test requires. More importantly, it relieves blacks of the need to develop them. Although the number of black firefighters may increase in the near term, the push to relax human capital requirements for education and employment is ultimately counterproductive. The black community should give up on deriding performance standards and attacking educational and job requirements. Efforts expended on relaxing such standards should be redirected towards meeting them. Indeed, if the energy invested in seeking exemptions were applied to improving skills, the payoff would be far greater in the long run. That is the strategy of choice for others from humble backgrounds, including many who start out with few resources and little ability to speak English. Once again, blacks will assert that racism distinguishes their case. But invoking generalized racism is unpersuasive without the identification of specific race-based factors that actually prevent blacks from playing by the rules that apply to everyone else.

10. Avoid Dwelling on the Past

A pervasive assumption of the discourse on race and racial disadvantage is that knowing how current inequalities came about is essential to figuring out how to eliminate them. Understanding how to move forward requires appreciating how we got here. Emblematic of this mentality is the juxtaposition in one issue of the *New York Times* of a story reporting inner-city black children's alarming failure rate on tests of basic scientific knowledge along with a prominent black columnist's op-ed piece lauding the documentary *Eyes on the Prize*.[29] Does this film celebrating the brave struggles of the civil rights era have anything whatsoever to tell us about how to raise these students' science scores? On reflection, the answer must be "no."

The assumption that the past informs the future helps explain the tenor of racial dialogue today. A conversation that begins as a forward-looking search for solutions soon degenerates into a backward-looking fixation on our nation's shameful history. Any suggestion that progress might require self-help inevitably gives rise to the accusation of blaming the victim. Talk of victim-blaming triggers an indignant insistence that society, and not the victim, is responsible for the present dilemma. This in turn generates a recital of the past wrongs that gave rise to the victim's predicament.

The tendency to revert to a rehearsal of historical oppression explains why discussions of racial justice often go nowhere. The exasperation of those who want to focus constructively on the future collides with the dudgeon of those who insist upon reviewing the roots of the current dilemma. As the participants talk past each other, they lose sight of a fundamental point: understanding historical antecedents often reveals little about cures. Yet the temptation to dwell on "root causes" is overwhelming. Ignoring the story of past crimes seems tantamount to denying responsibility for them. That notion is faulty. It proceeds from conflating liability with remedy.

Identifying the perpetrator and establishing the causal mechanism of harm need not point the way to an effective program of relief. The parable of the pedestrian illustrates this insight. A full description of the events leading to the pedestrian's injury will include information about his actions, the negligent driver's conduct, and the logistical details of the collision. Facts will emerge about the precise nature of the victim's physical injuries. But information about the sequence leading to harm—the account of injury—reveals nothing about how to proceed from injury to cure—the account of repair. The pedestrian's knowledge of the details of his accident does not teach him how to walk again. He must discover the drugs and therapies that will most effectively restore his function. He must master and practice the appropriate physical and therapeutic routines. He must do what is necessary to rehabilitate himself. Understanding how the accident occurred offers no help here.

A similar insight applies to racial justice. The myth of reverse causation assumes that the route out of inequality retraces the road in. If we understand how we arrived at the current juncture, we can devise solutions to the dilemma of race. But when harm takes the form of injuries to human capital, this assumption fails us. The path leading to harm and the path to reversing the harm can radically diverge. Not only may the agent of undoing be other than the wrongdoers, but knowing how the injury occurred rarely conveys anything useful about how to fix it. Accounts of how we arrived at our current state ultimately shed little light on what we should do about it.

Indeed, one of the frustrations inherent in the search for racial justice is that knowledge of the details of past persecution, although essential to establishing fault and responsibility, has not paid off in concrete solutions. Historical investigations have been remarkably unhelpful in the quest to alleviate present social problems. Nonetheless, it is widely assumed that behavior cannot be changed, modified, improved, or regulated without understanding its historical antecedents. But there is no evidence that eliminating racial disadvantage requires knowing its origins. No particular remedial recommendation necessarily follows from identifying past wrongdoing or describing past racial crimes. The very nature of the current shortfalls—which involve human capacities, outlook, and volition—resists illumination through this approach.

The literature on race relations is replete with historical accounts of how slavery weakened family ties by discouraging marriage among slaves and by dividing families. As an explanation for the precarious present state of the black family, this story is not entirely convincing. The black family was far more stable 50 years ago, when conditions for blacks were far worse than they are today. Black out-of-wedlock birth rates started to climb and marriage rates to fall around 1960, long after slavery was abolished and just as the civil rights movement gained momentum. Perhaps a more nuanced explanation for the recent deterioration is that the legacy of slavery made the black family more vulnerable to the cultural subversions of the 1960s. But what does this tell us that is useful today? The answer is: nothing. Examining the historical roots of father absence among blacks has not helped us to devise effective government programs to reduce it. Likewise, centuries of discrimination in jobs, education, and social life have generated relatively low levels of educational attainment and aspiration in the black community. But identifying these causes of educational under-achievement has not yielded a cure. The historical facts fail to reveal particular measures, whether programmatic or otherwise, for improving educational outcomes.

We know the historical causes very well. The solutions still elude us. Looking backward has not taught us much about how to go forward. This does not justify ignorance of the past. Historical understandings are important for moral clarity. They may foster group solidarity and fuel blacks' determination to address group problems. But beyond that, dwelling on the past offers little payoff and might even impede progress. By engendering false hopes of enlightenment, the historical record can distract from the task at hand. If the most fruitful solutions have little to do with the events that have brought the victims to their present juncture, then rehearsing racial wrongs will not likely reveal the best strategies. In devising a plan of action, the challenge is to figure out what works now and in the future. The task is to equip and induce people to take advantage of existing opportunities. History offers few lessons for achieving that goal.

11. Think Straight About Blaming the Victim

A central argument of this book is that accepting a key role for victims does not "blame the victim" because it implies no exoneration of the wrongdoer. As the parable of the pedestrian illustrates, relying on victims to heal their own injuries does not mean denying that others have harmed them.

Self-help advocates are repeatedly accused of blaming the victim. The argument here is that acknowledging the distinction between liability and remedy—between identifying the causes of problems and devising solutions—will help dissipate this accusation. But resistance to charging blacks with solving their own problems is not so easily overcome. It stems, in part, from confusion surrounding the language of praise and blame.

In ordinary English usage, "blaming the victim" is an ambiguous phrase. It can refer to assigning the victim a role in solving his own problems, regardless of their origins. But it also can mean assigning responsibility to the victim for causing his own problems in the first place. Conflating these two distinct ideas impedes clear thinking on race.

The argument here is that expecting blacks to repair the harms done to their group is appropriate, but absolving others of responsibility is not. Recognizing that society cannot fully undo the damage wrought by racism, and that blacks' active participation is indispensable, is not the same as denying that others are to blame for inflicting harm. Nor does it exempt society from doing as much as *effectively* possible to address racial inequality. Rather, it simply recognizes that the remedial ideal, which dictates that the wrongdoer correct all the damage done, cannot be realized in this instance.

Nonetheless, everyday language regularly threatens to collapse the distinction between accusing victims of causing harm and recognizing their role in correcting it. This is not surprising. Terms of blame and responsibility are routinely used to address both cause and remedy. Similar language is commonly employed to characterize both the wrongdoer's actions and the victim's self-repair.

To return to our central theme, suppose the injured pedestrian never does learn to walk again. He ignores the therapist's instructions and fails to exert the necessary effort. His friends might say that "it's his own fault" that he has not yet recovered. They might even say that "he has only himself to blame." They are indeed "blaming the victim" in the sense of charging him for his failure to heal himself. But the language people use to express dismay at the pedestrian's inadequate effort to address his own injuries sounds perilously close to expressing a very different (and false) idea: that the pedestrian's own conduct is the source of his problems in the first place, and the driver entirely blameless. Likewise, in the context of race, commonplace language that assigns responsibility for causes or cures is inherently ambiguous. This ambiguity gives rise to an understandable fear that proponents of self-help are denying historical reality—and to the conversation-stopping accusation of victim-blaming. It is important to resist this reaction and to recognize that those who look to victims to solve their own problems need not be denying others' past wrongs.

The conceptual confusion is not just a matter of linguistic imprecision and "loose talk." The term *blame* has a role in the ordinary discourse of self-help precisely because the practice of self-correction is not free from moral overtones. When, as with the injured pedestrian, a victim has no choice but to heal himself, it is natural to hold him responsible for doing so. It is a short step to faulting or "blaming" him for failing to discharge this role. Similarly, where the victim's behavior helps perpetuate his own debasement, it is not inappropriate to deplore his failure to take constructive action. Thus, although the language of blame can serve simply to acknowledge the victim's indispensable participation in his own recovery, it can also be used to express the judgment that the victim *should* help himself and that the victim who fails to do so is in some sense remiss. These normative implications follow naturally from seeing the victim as the gatekeeper of his own healing and as a free agent who can choose whether or not to make himself whole. This stance toward the victim is fully consistent with recognizing that others have caused the victim's injuries in the first place.[30]

Nonetheless, our commonplace language tends to muddy the distinction between liability and remedy. By threatening to collapse responsibility for causing harms and correcting harms, "blame talk" engenders the impression that focusing on the victim's remedial role is equivalent to exonerating wrongdoers or denying the reality of past racial persecution. This fuels hostility to self-help as the centerpiece of any program for racial justice. That response is misplaced. Recognizing a critical remedial role for victims need not absolve the wrongdoer. We should be vigilant against the confusions that undermine this important insight. The accusation of victim-blaming should not be permitted to silence the advocates of a fresh and forward-looking approach to racial inequality. It should not be allowed to fuel a return to the exhausted policies of the past, nor to impede a renewed focus on self-help.

||||||||||||||||||||||

The discussion up to this point has assumed the possibility of maintaining a crisp distinction between liability and remedy as applied to calls for racial justice. In taking that distinction seriously, it recommends looking forward rather than backward and shifting focus from causes to solutions. But can the separation of liability and remedy be so readily maintained? Is resistance to anything that smacks of blaming the victim just a product of confusion, or does the problem run far deeper? Is there anything to the objection that making self-help the centerpiece of efforts to achieve racial equality inevitably leads to denying society's responsibility for the present dilemma?

The argument so far has indeed finessed some hard questions. Social science and ordinary discourse have long grappled with fundamental issues regarding causation, choice, freedom, and justice for individuals who make poor choices or embrace maladaptive patterns in the wake of deprivation or adversity.[31] Whether past hardships doom or exonerate victims is an issue that arises in a broad array of contexts. As applied to race, the understanding that present social pathologies are the product of past mistreatment always raises the question of how we can expect group members to surmount these causal forces. The lockstep of causation has no evident stopping point: If past events brought victims to the present dilemma (so that they are, in some important sense, not responsible for it), how can those victims now be expected to rise above it?

It is here that reliance on human freedom—and the distinction between hard struggles and brick walls—come under great strain. The assumption that individuals retain the capacity to overcome the effects of historical persecution gives rise to a retrospective question: If we assume victims can surmount current difficulties prospectively, what do we make of their failure yet to do so? Because freedom to overcome does not arbitrarily begin in the present, the line between self-perpetuated dysfunction and self-inflicted wounds is not always sharp. If the chains can be broken today, why not yesterday? If the victim's efforts can work now and in the future, then perhaps they could have worked sooner. Indeed, does not the progress already made by a significant sector of the black community demonstrate that the potential for dramatic self-improvement has been present for some time? That possibility contains an implicit reproach. If the victims could have solved their own problems earlier but did not, it is hard to avoid assigning them at least some responsibility for the present dilemma. In this sense, remedy shades into liability, and the distinction between causing harms and fixing them threatens to break down.

This logic animates the thinking of those who would altogether absolve society of continuing responsibility for present racial disparities. According to this view, blacks' intervening choices, including the actions that perpetuate a dysfunctional culture, break the chain of causation and attenuate the fault of those who committed wrongs against blacks in the first place.[32] Although there may have been a time when blacks could blame others and claim recompense, they can now only blame themselves. In this view, outsiders owe nothing to the black community.

This argument is not the only one advanced by those who would minimize society's responsibility for the current problem of race. Recognizing the obligation to return blacks to the "rightful position" rests on determining what the rightful position is. This, in turn, requires constructing a counterfactual hypothetical about the position blacks would have occupied if the injury had not occurred.[33] Since many actions harmful to blacks are remote in time and complex in effect, this exercise is speculative at best and may be impossible. Alternatively, some argue that historical mistreatment left blacks no worse off. Without slavery, blacks would not be living in the United States, where everyone's life prospects are far better than in Africa.[34] Then there is the "nonidentity" problem, the argument that American blacks have really suffered no injury because, if their ancestors had not been enslaved, they would never have been born and thus would not even have *existed*.[35] There are yet other puzzles that implicate the collective and trans-generational nature of the claimed injuries. Most persons who engaged in active discrimination during historical periods of pervasive racism are no longer alive. This raises the question of why their children should pay for their sins. Likewise, it is not clear why persons who have not themselves engaged in discrimination should be charged with recompense,[36] or why those blacks whose ancestors were never enslaved should be compensated. For all these reasons, the continuing collective responsibility of white society for past, or even for present, racism and discrimination is controversial.

The point of this discussion is that whether blacks who fail to improve their own situation are in some sense "to blame" for racial inequality—and whether the rest of us are thereby exonerated—are not questions that can be wholly resolved by clearing up the conceptual confusions that are the focus of this book. Thus the wariness of those who resist the self-help approach is not wholly baseless. The distinction between responsibility and remedy can be slippery. There are some arguments for assigning remedial responsibility to victims that do imply diminished moral responsibility for others.

Some proponents of self-help may indeed believe that white society can no longer be charged with causing present racial inequality. How to respond to these concerns? First, the question of whether blacks' failure so far to engage in greater efforts to solve their own problems somehow attenuates others' responsibility is, at bottom, of minimal importance. Barriers for blacks until recently blocked almost all routes for advancement or constructive progress toward equality. Significant opportunities for self-betterment simply have not been available for very long—at most a few decades. These historical realities provide good reason to accept that others bear the bulk of the responsibility for blacks' present dilemma.

Second, one advantage of remedial realism is that it obviates the need to settle every thorny question regarding the roots of persistent racial disparities. The discussion has so far accepted that past official and unofficial discrimination are important sources of present black disadvantage. But a pragmatic remedial focus shows how controversies surrounding causation and responsibility need not actually be resolved. Indeed, the central contention here is that very little of practical significance now turns on whether society bears collective responsibility for blacks' current predicament. Nor does it make any difference whether past opportunities for self-help went unexploited. Regardless of how these questions are answered, the blueprint for *future* action remains the same. Racial equality depends on closing gaps in academic preparation, work, wealth, earnings, family structure, individual and community attitudes and practices, and the ability to thrive in a modern technological society. The victims' own behavior is the rate-limiting step: What really matters now is what blacks do for themselves. As a practical matter, this program requires nothing from outsiders save fair treatment, the opportunity to achieve a decent life, and the chance to advance through one's own efforts. These duties are not distinctly remedial. In our system, they are owed to everyone. Thus nothing of practical importance turns on whether past agents of oppression are more responsible than the victims themselves. In the end, what is important is what works and what does not.

Adopting a remedial focus that recognizes the centrality of self-help has the virtue of permitting what Cass Sunstein calls an "incompletely theorized agreement."[37] Because the program advocated here is entirely forward-looking, it sidesteps many points of disagreement in favor of developing a consensus about the most effective way to return the victim to a position of full equality. It also minimizes the need for completely resolving vexed and controversial questions about causation and responsibility in the profoundly divisive context of race.

Not all puzzles can be avoided, however. Two important remedial issues that arise in the quest for racial justice do directly implicate questions concerning societal responsibility. Those are reparations and affirmative action. Both require outsiders to take special and costly measures for the benefit of blacks. Deciding whether these remedies should be adopted makes it difficult to avoid considering the link between past mistreatment and present conditions. These topics are addressed in the next chapter.

CHAPTER 6

Reparations, Affirmative Action, and the Relationship of Race and Class

What About Reparations?

There is now a voluminous literature addressing whether reparations should be paid to black citizens for the harms of slavery and racial discrimination.[1] The issues are complex, with controversy centering on tracing the sources of victims' present deficits as well as on making people pay for the acts of past generations. There is one important aspect of remedies law, however, that is often overlooked in discussions of whether cash reparations for blacks would be appropriate: Money is the remedy of choice in just those cases where there is no action that the wrongdoer can effectively take to fully repair an injury. The courts routinely award damages (that is, monetary compensation) to victims for harms that cannot be completely undone through equitable (that is, nonmonetary) relief.

As the parable of the pedestrian illustrates, bodily harm is often just such a case. Indeed, physical injuries are sometimes permanent and irreversible. The victim can collect damages in those cases—and for wrongful death—even though money is not restorative. Indeed, monetary compensation, rather than equitable intervention, is the remedy of choice precisely because the wrongdoer cannot return the victim to his rightful position—that is, to his preinjured state. Because the harm can never be completely undone, cash is regarded as the appropriate relief.

The argument here is that racial wrongs are analogous. The legacies of past injuries are now shortfalls in personal and social capital that outsiders cannot effectively alleviate. But that is just where monetary awards make sense. On this view, reparations as a remedy for racial injustice comport with the more general remedial practice. Monetary relief is traditionally given precisely *because* the wrongdoer cannot restore the victim to his uninjured state. In those cases, money functions as relief of last resort. It is, in effect, a consolation prize. Thus, if societal responsibility for human capital injuries from racial discrimination is conceded, blacks would have a presumptive claim for racial reparations. This is so *even if* blacks— and blacks alone—ultimately possess the power to correct those problems for themselves.

That money can be an appropriate second-best remedy when other relief fails does not settle the issue. There are other arguments against reparations. As noted, some opponents deny society's responsibility altogether or argue that current taxpayers should not foot the bill for past sins. Others question the appropriateness of awards to all blacks, regardless of whether their ancestors were slaves. Although hotly contested in theory, some of these concerns have been downplayed or ignored in other contexts—for example, in the decision by Congress to pay reparations to Japanese Americans interned during World War II.

Leaving aside these questions, and regardless of whether remedial principles might otherwise support this form of relief, monetary compensation for racial injuries is destined to disappoint. As with other outside interventions designed to address racial gaps, there is no guarantee that granting reparations would reduce lingering inequality and sound reasons to expect that it will not achieve this result. Cash transfers may transiently reduce poverty, but decades of experience with welfare have shown that such measures are as likely to be adverse as beneficial. Money will not necessarily alleviate the black-white academic achievement gap. Nor is it likely that cash awards for blacks will increase the popularity of marriage, reduce extramarital childbearing, alter the crime rate, or otherwise significantly improve black Americans' earnings, accomplishments, or job prospects. Given the unique nature of human capital injuries, it is a mistake to expect that placing more money in people's hands will suffice to erase stubborn racial disparities. Although hope springs eternal that compensation will in fact compensate, money has no proven effect on behavior. It does not guarantee a new outlook or greater effort. It does not ensure that talent will be developed. Indeed, reparations will almost certainly achieve very little. As the parable of the pedestrian illustrates, money is ineffective if the victim's failure to act limits progress. Since this is arguably where we stand today with race, throwing money at the problem will not correct the present imbalance in group outcomes.

Nonetheless, compensation might still be warranted and could have some beneficial effects. Ideally, cash transfers would shift the focus of remediation to victims and would spotlight victims' choices. Reparations could provide the occasion for realizing that what blacks do with the money is far more important than the money itself. On the other hand, one potentially undesirable consequence of reparations, as with other remedial programs, is that disappointing results might fuel open-ended or escalating demands for additional compensation. If reparations fail to change blacks' situation, that might be taken as proof that the amounts paid are insufficient. Obviously, whether reparations in fact correct the harms attributed to past wrongs should not be used as the measure of their adequacy. Any program of reparations should be kept well within bounds.

This discussion also has implications for private giving designed to help improve the situation of blacks. Nothing here counsels against charities providing funds to black persons or community organizations for a variety of projects and purposes. Ideally, that money would be devoted to helping those who help themselves. The danger with any outside assistance—whether public or private, monetary or in-kind—is that it invites a focus on doing things *to* people and *for* people. Efforts directed at accomplishing what people can only do for themselves run the risk of engendering passivity and distracting from the needed emphasis on self-help. Because others' contributions can never substitute for victims' doing their part, private interventions, like public ones, are often doomed to disappointment and failure.

What About Affirmative Action?

Race-based affirmative action has been analyzed in voluminous detail, and a full explication is beyond the scope of this inquiry. Specifically, this discussion does not deal with the goal of diversity that has recently been asserted to justify affirmative action, especially in education. That rationale is only tenuously connected to remedial purposes. A defense of affirmative action as relief for past and present injuries, however, requires accepting present collective responsibility for racial inequality. As with reparations, the remedial case for affirmative action requires resolving hard questions of historical and social causation.

The position advanced here, which is that self-help must now be the chief strategy for eliminating lingering racial disparities, implies that affirmative action is both unnecessary and ineffective. Because, by definition, affirmative-action programs give blacks something they could not obtain in the current system through their own devices, such programs assume that racial equality requires special outside intervention. Like some other programs that stress targeted external assistance, however, affirmative action is not necessarily inconsistent with *some* role for victims in self-healing. Rather, proponents may believe that opportunities over and above a "level playing field" are needed for self-help to be effective.

At first blush, affirmative action appears to satisfy mainstream remedial principles. After all, the goal is to return blacks to the position they would have occupied in the absence of discrimination. On closer examination, there are two distinct ways to think about affirmative action's restorative goals. In one view, undoing the harm of discrimination means directly placing persons in positions they would have occupied but for the inflicted injuries. If decades of racism and discrimination have prevented blacks from becoming doctors, lawyers, business owners, or teachers, then we must ensure by *force majeure*, or whatever means necessary, that more blacks come to occupy these positions.

An alternative view is that the goal should not just be placing persons in particular positions, but ensuring that they can attain those positions by the ordinary route, under their own steam, and without special help. The ultimate objective is to transform victims into people who can compete for social rewards by dint of their own efforts on a par with members of other groups.

The first type of affirmative action is a distinctly inferior remedy. Since it does not include erasing the human capital injuries that are a principal legacy of racism, it is partial and incomplete. In contrast, a true "make-whole" remedy would entirely eliminate whatever underlying deficits contribute to disparate outcomes, including any cultural and behavioral differences that undermine the ability to compete on terms of strict equality with other races. By this criterion, the second type of affirmative action comes closer to fulfilling the remedial ideal.

On this second view of affirmative action, equality would eventually become self-sustaining. Once the group differences at issue disappeared, the need for affirmative action would as well. Blacks would be independently capable of keeping up with others. Affirmative action in this model would, by definition, be temporary and affirmative action programs would be allowed to expire. In contrast, without such enduring improvements, *the need for affirmative action would continue indefinitely* and perpetual intervention would be required. These insights underlie some judges' assertions that affirmative action programs, as properly conceived, should "sunset," or cease to be necessary, at some future point.[2] The expectation that such remedies will eventually end is not just an effort to limit their cost. Rather, it comes directly out of a basic remedial principle. Perpetual affirmative action programs necessarily fall short of make-whole relief. In effect, the damage is not fully repaired until reparative efforts cease to be necessary. That extra help is no longer needed is, in fact, the true test of whether relief is complete. At that point, the remedial ideal has been achieved.

From the point of view of standard remedies doctrine alone, the inferior form of affirmative action—affirmative action by perpetual *force majeure*—is not *per se* unacceptable. An incomplete remedy is better than none. But affirmative action as a limitless intervention does have severe drawbacks: It carries ongoing costs in inefficiency and potential unfairness to those displaced by racial assignment to sought-after positions. The fuller conception of affirmative action imposes such costs only transiently. That is often cited as one reason why a complete and self-sustaining remedy should be the ultimate goal.

In deciding whether such an objective can be achieved, the pertinent question for our purposes is whether reverse discrimination is an *effective* remedy for racial disparities. Will affirmative action return blacks to their rightful position in the fullest sense by eventually eliminating the need for it? Will it erase the most important deficits currently holding blacks back—those that implicate human capital and behavior? Affirmative action programs rest on the assumption that equality *cannot* be achieved without going beyond a "level playing field" and that access to meritocratic positions in schools and the workplace must be made easier. Is there reason to believe both that this easier access is necessary to eliminate remaining disparities and that it will actually work to do so?

A central tenet of affirmative action is that the advantages it confers will eventually correct the conditions that make it necessary. In this respect, it potentially suffers from the same weakness as other programmatic approaches targeted at similar deficits: It assumes that an externally engineered fix can work fundamental changes in behavior.

Although disagreement rages on whether affirmative action can in fact make good on this promise, the evidence is not encouraging. As practiced so far, such initiatives have not done much to close or even significantly narrow overall social and economic gaps between blacks and others. There are many methodological problems with assessing the efficacy of affirmative action, including the difficulty of documenting the extent to which it is practiced in education, employment, or other sectors, and the uncertainty regarding the criteria for success. Because the data suggest that reverse discrimination is particularly strong in education, especially at the college level, how blacks admitted to college under affirmative-action programs fare after graduation has been an intensive subject of investigation and controversy.[3] But the larger question of whether educational affirmative action is actually working to correct stark racial imbalances in academic accomplishment and college attendance overall has received much less attention.

There is as yet little persuasive evidence that affirmative action programs improve the very educational deficits for which they are designed to compensate. As already discussed, the data indicate that lack of academic preparation is the principal reason for blacks' continuing low rates of college attendance and completion. Although affirmative action might influence the specific institutions black students attend, it appears to have had no positive effect on preschool, grade-school, and high-school achievement overall. Nor have decades of affirmative action significantly narrowed the stubborn performance differences among Asian, white, and black students from every social class that are uniformly observed nationwide. After initial progress in closing test-score gaps between the 1960s and 1980s, disparities by race have held steady or increased and remain wide. Even among elite minority students who most benefit from educational affirmative-action initiatives, there has been no real progress. As a comprehensive review of race in higher education recently noted, "the underrepresentation of blacks in the top tenth of the test-score distribution has not changed in recent decades," and there is "no basis for being optimistic about [future] score convergence."[4] In sum, if group equality in educational outcomes is the goal, affirmative action to date has not worked and shows little promise of working in the future. Indeed, the evidence is consistent with the opposite effect. Black students from educated and affluent families lag even further behind their white counterparts than less privileged students.[5] These observations suggest that, by lowering barriers to entry, affirmative action may depress minority precollege effort and achievement.

Similar observations are in order for affirmative action on the job. Because there are fewer reliable benchmarks than for education, it is even harder to know how extensive is the practice in employment. Although some economists have tried to show that affirmative-action hires are no less productive than other workers,[6] good evidence that affirmative action on the job is actually working to close gaps across a range of social and economic indicators is hard to find. There is little reliable information available on the connection between affirmative action in employment and other "supply side" trends, such as family stability or the development of skills in very young children, that drive economic and social inequality.

Perhaps the most persuasive argument for affirmative action in education and employment is that benefits will only be felt in the longer term. Over time, access to better schools and jobs will raise blacks' income and enhance exposure to mainstream values and elite culture. This will, in turn, shape habits of work, leisure, family, and childrearing. As affirmative action propels individuals into the middle or upper class, beneficiaries will adopt attitudes and behaviors that will effect changes over generations. If these eventually become self-sustaining, racial inequalities will disappear.

This scenario cannot be dismissed, but it remains highly speculative. Most of blacks' economic and social gains in the past century cannot be ascribed to affirmative-action programs, which post-date the most dramatic improvements. The changes that are now needed are those that will upgrade black student achievement, decrease the number of crimes blacks commit, and enhance their performance as workers and entrepreneurs. The link between these desired outcomes and affirmative action is tenuous at best. Right now, affirmative action is a policy that disproportionately benefits the best students and workers. Because the deficits that hold blacks back show up early, cut across all classes, and are most evident among those who are scarcely touched by affirmative action at all, the prediction that such programs will generate behavioral changes that significantly reduce or eliminate group inequalities is implausible.

In sum, just as there is no good evidence that stamping out present discrimination will work enduring changes in the current situation for blacks, so also is there little reason to believe that affirmative action will bring about self-sustaining racial equality. Although affirmative action propels more blacks to desirable positions, the operation of current programs is closer to the second-best model of never-ending *force majeure* than to the temporary, but complete and enduring, relief that is the ideal remedy. Remedial principles do not rule out recourse to half-measure affirmative action, and such programs may or may not justify the costs. But if affirmative action does not eventually prove self-sustaining, its justification is seriously undermined.

But perhaps the most compelling reason to de-emphasize affirmative action is that such programs are fundamentally at odds with a key aspect of self-betterment, which is the rejection of double standards.[7] Attacking education or job requirements impedes progress toward the core goal of equality, which is that blacks become as qualified as everyone else. As already noted, it is especially important to embrace expectations that bear on the development of human capital. Efforts should be made not to lower standards, but to meet them.

Race and Class

This book has addressed the gap in average social and economic position between a historically oppressed group, American blacks, and others in American society. In its focus on race rather than class, it does not offer a commentary on the problems of poverty, disadvantage, and social inequality in general. The question at issue is not why there is economic inequality in our society and what, if anything, should be done about it, but why one race lags systematically behind others on important fronts and how that problem can best be solved.

The argument that present racial inequality will only yield to self-help entails no particular position on the obligation of government or private actors to address the causes or effects of economic inequality overall. It is consistent with a larger or smaller welfare state or more or less redistribution through tax and transfer programs designed to narrow income differences or improve the well-being of the least well off. Nonetheless, an economic safety net, even if extensive, is not and cannot be a grand program for social engineering. It cannot transform race relations or erase disparities by class. Thus, the analysis here does assume that some degree of inequality will continue to be a feature of our economic life and that persons in each ethnic and racial group will span a spectrum of economic and social well-being.

Although the problems of racial inequality and economic inequality share common elements, they are distinct in key respects. First, not all group claims for assistance are equally compelling. The phenomenon of ethnic and racial inequality exists worldwide with some groups lagging significantly in different societies.[8] The causes of such stratification are often complex and not easily traceable to overt mistreatment, persecution, or discrimination. Within market-based societies characterized by political and economic competition, group differences in success need not result from invidious action. Rather, these patterns may arise spontaneously from the interplay of systemic demands, disparate starting points, and cultural differences in practice, orientation, beliefs, and values.

The remedial framework is therefore not appropriate for addressing all group disparities or for reducing economic disadvantage as a whole. Rather, it fits best where distinct groups have been the clear targets of sustained discrimination or persecution. Where group differences cannot be viewed as resulting from such insults, there is no reason to conclude that assistance is owed as a matter of *remedial* justice.

Societies may nonetheless have principled or pragmatic reasons to mitigate economic inequality through the redistribution of opportunities or resources. Some liberal theorists embrace a form of luck egalitarianism, which holds individuals responsible for bad choices but recognizes society's obligation to compensate for deficient natural endowments or other uncontrollable misfortunes.[9] There are also sound political reasons to reduce economic inequalities, as extremes of wealth and poverty can undermine the functioning of democratic institutions.[10]

It is paradoxical that self-help may be a more effective strategy for closing gaps between racial groups than for mitigating poverty or economic inequality generally. The overall distribution of resources is mainly the product of economic structure and political choices.[11] In the United States, earnings and wealth have recently become less equal, with globalization of capital and labor, the decline of labor unions, growing returns to skill and education, and higher costs for housing, education, and health care, all thought to contribute to increased economic polarization. Taxes and public benefits programs also affect resource distribution. These factors lie beyond the direct control of particular persons or social groups and are largely independent of their values and behavior.

The overall shape of the economy is thus mainly the product of larger forces. Nonetheless, an individual's own economic well-being is not completely outside his control. How persons fare within the existing economic structure often depends on individual choices, such as whether to pursue an education, live prudently, work steadily, or get married.[12] But this observation illustrates why achieving equality for blacks is no longer primarily a task for politics but rather a matter of personal behavior. The question of black equality is one of blacks' relative position within the existing society. Blacks could catch up to others without any significant changes in the general reward structure. Such a development would require only that blacks occupy a different mix of positions than they do at present. In this respect, achieving equality for a particular race is a fundamentally different goal from reducing economic disparities in society as a whole or increasing the well-being of the least advantaged overall. The latter projects are not so much designed to enhance people's ability to compete or to guarantee their success as to protect them from the failure to do so. Because blacks are disproportionately poor, they may benefit relatively more than others from policies designed to help alleviate economic hardship. But, given the nature of present disparities, such assistance will not ensure that blacks catch up with other groups.

To be sure, the health of the system and the choices individuals make within it cannot be so neatly separated. Consider family structure, which has diverged dramatically by class and race over the past few decades. This divergence has exacerbated inequalities in society as a whole. If families at the bottom of the income scale were stronger and more stable, family income might become less dispersed and current economic disparities might shrink. Educational choices also influence the shape and vigor of the economy. Declines in the dropout rate or increases in learning or achievement can shape economic development and overall prosperity by allowing expansion in areas that draw on skilled labor. Finally, the importance of culturally conditioned behavior to economic health can be observed worldwide. Consider, for example, the Scandinavian countries' signal success in maintaining economic growth while simultaneously reducing inequality and poverty.[13] Although economic policies and generous social programs have undeniably played some role, a culture that fosters social order, skill development, and solidarity has surely been important as well.

There is no shortage of proposals designed to address the problems of poverty and economic inequality, including expanding the Earned Income Tax Credit, bolstering unemployment insurance, raising the minimum wage, and increasing access to health care. These problems have acquired new urgency in light of the recent economic crisis and the advent of recession. But general programs to aid the disadvantaged and assist the middle class will not necessarily reduce racial inequality because all groups can benefit proportionally, leaving stubborn racial disparities in place.[14] Consider, for example, the idea of universal preschool education, which has recently received widespread attention.[15] Programs like this often suffer from a confusion about goals. Is the objective to close racial gaps, enhance poor children's opportunities, or assist families? Although more and better preschool will help those at the bottom, it may not change the fact that blacks are overrepresented in that group. In summary, that the government might have a significant role to play in alleviating poverty and securing economic opportunity does not mean that it can do much to close racial gaps. Racial and economic inequality are, in important respects, different problems with distinct origins and solutions.

Conclusion

This book argues that self-correction and internal cultural reform are now the only effective tactics for eliminating black disadvantage. This position meets opposition from many quarters. Ordinary citizens and civil rights advocates resist the self-help message. Legal advocates reject it on the grounds of injustice, and social scientists on the basis of theoretical unsoundness. Remedial idealism and sociological thinking fuel this hostility. Societal oppression brought blacks to this situation, so it is up to society to fix what is broken. Looking to blacks to solve their own problems is fundamentally unjust and delusional. Their situation is the product of outside forces, so they cannot improve it nor can we expect them to. These notions impede clear thinking about black Americans' present dilemma and future prospects.

Blacks continue to lag behind others on critical dimensions of social and economic well-being. The dominant view is that racial inequality can only be eliminated by eradicating racism and providing effective, well-funded social programs. This book uses core concepts from the law of remedies to argue that breaking the stalemate on how best to respond to persistent racial disparities requires dispelling the confusion surrounding blacks' own role in achieving equality. The legal doctrine of remedies recognizes a sharp distinction between liability, or the cause of a harm, and remedy, which encompasses undoing that harm. Although the wrongdoer must repair any injury he has caused, the law recognizes that this is not always possible. In some cases, only the victim can make himself whole. The parable of the injured pedestrian illustrates this insight. The pedestrian's own efforts are critical to his recovery. If he fails to play his role, others' assistance will make no difference.

This point applies to the present dilemma of black disadvantage. Social science evidence shows that dysfunctional behaviors and the inadequate development of human capital, not discrimination, are now the most important factors holding blacks back. The nature of persistent disparities, as well as experience with interventions designed to address them, reveals that outsiders' power to change existing patterns is severely limited. The strategies of the past have exhausted themselves and can no longer work. The future of black America is now in its own hands.

NOTES

Introduction

1. William Ryan, *Blaming the Victim* (New York: Pantheon Books, 1971), at xiii; 24.
2. Erik Eckholm, "Plight Deepens for Black Men, Studies Warn," *The New York Times,* 20 March 2006, sec. A1; see also Orlando Patterson, "Culture and the Fate of Black Men," *The New York Times,* 2 April 2006, sec. 4, p. 11; Orlando Patterson, "A Poverty of the Mind," *The New York Times,* 26 March 2006, §4, at 13.
3. For accounts and discussion of these statements, see, e.g., Felicia R. Lee, "Cosby Defends His Remarks About Poor Blacks' Values," *The New York Times,* 22 May 2004, sec. B7.
4. See, e.g., Michael Eric Dyson, *Is Bill Cosby Right: Or Has the Black Middle Class Lost Its Mind?* (New York: Basic Civitas Books, 2005); Leonard Pitts, Jr., "Failing To Recognize the Effects of Racism," *The Philadelphia Inquirer,* 22 May 2006, sec. A15; Hamil R. Harris, "Some Blacks Find Nuggets of Truth in Cosby's Speech," *WashingtonPost.com,* 26 May 2004, sec. B5; Thomas Sowell, "Bravo for Bill Cosby," *Townhall.com,* 25 May 2004.
5. Juan Williams, *Enough* (New York: Crown Publishers, 2006); William H. Cosby, Jr. and Alvin F. Poussaint, *Come On, People: On the Path from Victims to Victors* (Nashville: Thomas Nelson, 2007). See also John McWhorter, *Losing the Race: Self-Sabotage in Black America* (New York: The Free Press, 2000); *Winning the Race: Beyond the Crisis in Black America* (New York: Gotham Books, 2005); Shelby Steele, *The Content of Our Character* (New York: HarperCollins, 1991).

Chapter 1: The Remedial Ideal and the Demand for Racial Justice

1. Specifically, some have suggested that existing patterns are at least partly a holdover from native African ways of life that preceded the slave era. See, e.g., J. Philippe Rushton, *Race, Evolution, and Behavior* (New Brunswick, N.J.: Transaction, 2000).

2. For a classic statement of the "rightful position" in conjunction with the make-whole ideal in Anglo-Saxon law, see Douglas Laycock, *Modern American Remedies* (New York: Aspen, 2002), p. 12 ("The fundamental principle of [monetary relief] is to restore the injured party, as nearly as possible, to the position he would have been in had it not been for the wrong of the other party."); and p. 281 (injunctions should, at a minimum, "restore the plaintiff as near as may be to the position it would have occupied but for the violation"). See also David S. Schoenbrod, "The Measure of an Injunction: A Principle to Replace Balancing the Equities and Tailoring the Remedy," *Minnesota Law Review* 72 (April 1988): 628 (noting the core principle that injunctive or equitable remedies aim to "restore the position that the plaintiff would have had but for the wrong—'plaintiff's rightful position.'").

3. Because some injuries arise from complex chains of events and implicate multiple actors, determining what position the victim would have occupied if the injury had not occurred is speculative and fraught with uncertainties. For harms remote in time, it may be especially unclear how events would have played out had the wrongs never been inflicted. In some cases, intervening events cast doubt on the alleged wrongdoer's sole responsibility and duty to provide full relief. The innocent choices of third parties, or decisions taken on the part of the victims themselves, may make the rightful position hard to discern. As discussed more extensively later in this book, these issues have particular salience in the historical context of race. On the difficulties that arise in constructing the counterfactual hypothetical necessary to define the elements of "make whole" relief for racial harms, see generally Kim Forde-Mazrui, "Taking Conservatives Seriously: A Moral Justification for Affirmative Action and Reparations," *California Law Review* 92 (2004): 685. See generally Cass R. Sunstein, "The Limits of Compensatory Justice" in *Compensatory Justice* (New York: New York University Press, 1991), pp. 281–310.

4. See, e.g., Ronnie Janoff-Bulman, *Shattered Assumptions: Towards a New Psychology of Trauma* (New York: The Free Press, 1992); James A. Chu, *Rebuilding Shattered Lives: The Responsible Treatment of Complex Post-Traumatic and Dissociative Disorders* (New York: John Wiley & Sons, 1998).

5. These observations apply to other forms of deprivation and injury as well. See, e.g., Stephen J. Morse, "Deprivation and Desert," in William C. Heffernan and J. Kleinig (eds.), *From Social Justice to Criminal Justice: Poverty and the Administration of Criminal Law,* Vol. 114 (New York: Oxford University Press, 2000), p. 130.

Chapter 2: Group Disadvantage and the Case of Race

1. See Lawrence E. Harrison and Samuel P. Huntington, *Culture Matters: How Values Shape Human Progress* (New York: Basic Books, 2000); Amy Chua, *World on Fire: How Exporting Free Market Democracy Breeds Ethnic Hatred and Global Instability* (New York: Doubleday, 2003); Thomas Sowell, *Race and Culture: A World View* (New York: Basic Books, 1994).

2. See Daryl Michael Scott, *Social Policy and the Image of the Damaged Black Psyche, 1880–1996* (Chapel Hill, N.C.: The University of North Carolina Press, 1997); Orlando Patterson, *Rituals of Blood: Consequences of Slavery in Two American Centuries* (Washington, D.C.: Civitas/CounterPoint, 1998); Elijah Anderson, *Code of the Streets: Decency, Violence, and the Moral Life of the Inner City* (New York: Norton, 1999). Nonetheless, this view is not embraced universally. Especially with respect to family structure, some resist the notion of black dysfunction. See discussion in Chapter 2, infra.

3. For an interesting summary of the controversies surrounding collective responsibility for group harms over generations, see George Sher, "Transgenerational Compensation," *Philosophy and Public Affairs* 33 (Spring 2005). On causation, liability, and compensation for complex social harms in the context of race, see Kim Forde-Mazrui, "Taking Conservatives Seriously: A Moral Justification for Affirmative Action and Reparations," *California Law Review* 92 (2004): 685. See also Cass R. Sunstein, "The Limits of Compensatory Justice" in *Compensatory Justice* (New York: New York University Press, 1991), 281–310. These issues are critical to the dispute surrounding reparations for racial harms. See Alfred Brophy, "Reconstructing Reparations," *Indiana Law Journal* 81 (2006). See also the discussion of reparations in Chapter 6.

4. See Chapter 3.

5. On the just world bias, see M. J. Lerner and D. T. Miller, "Just World Research and Attribution Process: Looking Back and Ahead," *Psychological Bulletin* 85 (1978): 1030–1051, and M. Lerner, *The Belief in a Just World: A Fundamental Delusion* (New York: Plenum, 1980).

6. See Douglas Massey and Nancy Denton, *American Apartheid: Segregation and the Making of the Underclass* (Cambridge: Harvard University Press, 1993); Michael Eric Dyson, *Is Bill Cosby Right: Or Has the Black Middle Class Lost Its Mind?* (New York: Basic Civitas Books, 2005).

7. There is a growing scholarly literature that purports to document the existence of inadvertent, unconscious racial bias and touts its growing

importance in maintaining racial disparities. See Jerry Kang, "Trojan Horses of Race," *Harv. L. Rev.* 118 (2005): 1491, 1537; Ian Ayres, *Pervasive Prejudice: Unconventional Evidence of Race and Gender Discrimination* (Chicago: University of Chicago Press, 2001); but see Amy L. Wax, "Discrimination as Accident," *Indiana Law J.* 47 (Fall 1999): 1129; Amy L. Wax, "The Discriminating Mind: Define It, Prove It," *Connecticut Law Review* 40 (2008): 979. See discussion in Chapter 3.

8. See Glenn C. Loury, *One by One from the Inside Out: Essays and Reviews on Race and Responsibility in America* (New York: The Free Press, 1995); Daria Roithmayr, "Locked in Segregation," *The Virginia Journal of Social Policy & the Law* 12, 2 (Winter 2004): 197–259.

9. For a recent statement of the structural racism thesis, see Olatunde C. A. Johnson, "Disparity Rules," 107 *Columbia Law Review* 374 (2007): 381, 385. According to Johnson, many current racial disparities are "the vestige of an inherited unjust social order" rather than "something produced by current policies."

10. See Jerry Kang, "Trojan Horses of Race," 1491, 1537.

11. See Ian Ayres, *Pervasive Prejudice?*.

12. See Michael Fix and Raymond J. Struyk, eds., *Clear and Convincing Evidence: Measurement of Discrimination in America* (Washington, D.C.: Urban Institute Press, 1993); Ian Ayres, "Fair Driving: Gender and Race Discrimination in Retail Car Negotiations," *Harvard Law Review* 104 (1991): 817.

13. For an early work in this tradition, see Lee Rainwater, *Behind Ghetto Walls* (Chicago: Aldine, 1970). More recently, see Christopher Jencks, *Rethinking Social Policy: Race, Poverty, and the Underclass* (Cambridge: Harvard University Press, 1992); William Julius Wilson, *The Truly Disadvantaged* (Chicago: University of Chicago Press, 1987); Elijah Anderson, *Code of the Street: Decency, Violence, and the Moral Life of the Inner City* (New York: Norton, 1999); Orlando Patterson, *Rituals of Blood* (New York: Basic Books, 1998). See also Belinda Tucker and Claudia Mitchell-Kernan, *The Decline in Marriage Among African-Americans* (New York: Russell Sage Foundation, 1995).

14. See Thomas Sowell, *Black Rednecks and White Liberals* (San Francisco: Encounter Books, 2005).

15. He is not alone among black sociologists in identifying a distinct ghetto culture. See also Elijah Anderson, *Code of the Streets;* Cornel West, *Race Matters* (Boston: Beacon Press, 1993).

16. For a characteristic statement along these lines, see J. D. Greenstone, "Culture, Rationality and the Underclass," in *The Urban Underclass,* Chris-

topher Jencks and Paul E. Peterson, eds. (Washington, D.C.: The Brookings Institution, 1991). See also Linda M. Burton, "Teenage Childbearing as an Alternative Life-Course Strategy in Multigeneration Black Families," *Human Nature* 1 (1990): 123–143.

17. On the dichotomy between character discourse and a circumstantial or sociological view, see David Brooks, "Virtues and Victims," *New York Times,* 9 April 2006, sec. 4, p. 12; David Brooks, "The Morality Line," *New York Times,* 19 April 2007, A27. See also John M. Doris, *Lack of Character: Personality and Moral Behavior* (Cambridge: Cambridge University Press, 2002).

18. Lawrence Harrison, *The Central Liberal Truth* (New York: Oxford University Press, 2006), 12; Luigo Guiso, Paola Sapienza, and Luigi Zingales, "Does Culture Affect Economic Outcomes?," *J. of Economic Perspectives* 20 (Spring 2006): 46. (Posing the unresolved questions of "How does culture emerge and how does it persist?" and "What is the interaction between culture and formal institutions?"). For more discussion of culture and the possibility of self-initiated cultural reform, see Chapter 5.

19. Harrison, *The Central Liberal Truth,* 1.

20. For a classic commentary on deterministic explanations—and excuses—for behavioral disadvantage, see Paul Hollander, "Sociology, Selective Determinism, and the Rise of Expectations," *American Sociologist* 8 (1973): 147. According to Hollander, "Sociological determinism is generously but selectively applied to excuse, mitigate, or condemn different forms of behavior or even the same behavior on the part of different people or groups. . . . [o]nly the behavior of 'underdogs' is socially determined, . . . [and] only people assigned to such groups are not in full control of their lives and behavior." Hollander sees this thinking as simultaneously satisfying the need for a systematic "scientific" model of behavior while also vindicating a left-leaning worldview: "Sociology stresses the social over the personal, the group rather than the individual, social forces over personal motives, the patterned instead of the unique, and the determined rather than the undetermined aspects of social existence. Not only does such an orientation follow from the most obvious and fundamental premises of the discipline, but it is also intimately related to the liberal political values and social consciousness of most sociologists."

21. Proponents of situationism frequently rely on the literature documenting a "fundamental attribution error," the tendency when evaluating others to overestimate the importance of personal characteristics and underestimate the role of circumstances. See John M. Doris, *Lack of Character: Personality and Moral Behavior* (Cambridge: Cambridge Univer-

sity Press, 2002) reviewing social psychological evidence on the role of dispositions and situational influence. See also Daniel Gilbert et al., eds., *The Handbook of Social Psychology,* 4th ed. (New York: Oxford University Press, 1998). This reliance is both conceptually and factually misplaced. That people sometimes err in estimating the relative importance of individual traits and circumstances to behavior does not mean that differences in character or personality are illusory or that they play no role in human conduct. See Natalie Gold, "What Is a Character Trait?" www.unc.edu/~gsmunc/EthicsGroup/WhatIsACharacterTrait.pdf. Nor does the fact that people sometimes respond similarly to circumstances mean that they are not responsible for their choices or that they are incapable of choosing otherwise. And, in fact, people do indeed show a range of reactions to similar constraints. On situationism generally, see Philip Zimbardo, *Lucifer Effect: Understanding How Good People Turn Evil* (New York: Random House, 2007). For a critique of Zimbardo, see Cass R. Sunstein, "The Thin Line," *The New Republic* 236 (May 21, 2007), pp. 51–55.

22. See Walter Mischel and P. K. Peake, "Beyond Deja Vu in the Search for Cross-Situational Consistency," *Psychological Review* 89 (1982): 730–755 demonstrating consistency in conscientious behaviors. See also Natalie Gold, "What is a Character Trait?" 19 ff. discussing intragroup and intergroup differences in behavior under experimental conditions and reviewing evidence that personality measures predict behavior; also p. 30 discussing the social science debate over the existence of stable behavioral traits. See also Daniel J. Ozer and Veronica Benet-Martinez, "Personality and the Prediction of Consequential Outcomes," *Ann. Rev. of Psychol.* 57 (2006): 401–421; David Lubinski, "Scientific and Social Significance of Assessing Individual Differences: 'Sinking Shafts at a Few Critical Points,'" *Ann. Rev. of Psychol.* 51 (2000): 405–444; Walter Mischel, "Toward an Integrative Science of the Person," *Ann Rev. of Psychol.* 55 (2004): 1–22.

23. See, for example, Orlando Patterson, "A Poverty of the Mind," *The New York Times,* 26 March 2006, sec. 4, p. 13.

24. For works that stress the primacy of self-help, see Dinesh d'Souza, *The End of Racism* (New York: The Free Press, 1995); Shelby Steele, *The Content of Our Character: A New Vision of Race in America* (New York: St. Martin's Press, 1990); John McWhorter, *Winning the Race* (New York: Gotham Books, 2005). See also Juan Williams, *Enough* (New York: Crown Publishers, 2006).

25. See the discussion on economic class and race in Chapter 6.

26. See Peter Edelman, Harry J. Holzer, and Paul Offner, *Reconnecting Disadvantaged Young Men* (Washington, D.C.: Urban Institute Press, 2006); see also Ronald B. Mincy, ed., *Black Males Left Behind* (Washington, D.C.: Urban Institute Press, 2006). For an up-to-date review of the state of black America that calls for renewed interventions to address continuing deficits in employment and educational achievement as well as high rates of crime and family disintegration, see Douglas S. Massey and Robert J. Sampson, "The Moynihan Report Revisited: Lessons and Reflections after Four Decades," *Annals of the American Academy of Political and Social Science* 621 (January 2009).

27. See Kathryn Edin and Maria Kefalas, *Promises I Can Keep* (Berkeley: University of California Press, 2005). For further discussion, see Chapter 3.

28. Edin and Kefalas, *Promises I Can Keep,* 217–218.

29. See Amy Wax, "Too Few Good Men," *Policy Review* 134 (Dec. 2005 & Jan. 2006): 69–79.

30. Lawrence Harrison makes a similar point from an internationalist perspective, noting that "in multicultural countries where the economic opportunities and incentives are available to all, some ethnic or religious minorities do much better than majority populations." See Lawrence Harrison, *The Central Liberal Truth,* 12.

31. Stephan Thernstrom and Abigail Thernstrom, *America in Black and White: One Nation, Indivisible* (New York: Touchstone, 1999).

32. Daniel P. Moynihan, Timothy M. Smeeding, and Lee Rainwater, eds., *The Future of the Family* (New York: Russell Sage Publications, 2004), xvii, citing Peter Rossi, "The Iron Law of Evaluation and Other Metallic Roles," in Joann L. Miller and Michael Lewis, eds., 4 *Research in Social Problems and Public Policy* (Greenwich, CT: JAI Press, 1987), 4.

33. Of course, dysfunctional behaviors could be addressed by *force majeure.* A totalitarian government could require persons to marry or to work. It could forbid or punish out-of-wedlock childbearing or other forms of ill-advised behavior. But our society leaves these types of decisions to private choice and therefore forgoes the option of undoing these effects of past discrimination by force.

34. See Iris M. Young, "Making Single Motherhood Normal" *Dissent* 41 (Winter 1994): 88–93.

35. See, for example, "'Live' with TAE: Interview with Shelby Steele," *American Enterprise Magazine* (April 2006), 12–17. John McWhorter, *Winning*

the Race (New York: Gotham Books, 2005); Juan Williams, "Getting Past Katrina," *The New York Times,* 1 September 2006, A17.

36. For more discussion of cultural reform, see Chapter 5.

37. For a discussion of the relationship of policies designed to achieve racial equality and those promoting economic security, see Chapter 6.

38. See the discussion in Chapter 6.

39. This three-part formula for escaping poverty, which was first proposed by Isabel Sawhill and Christopher Jencks, has recently been restated by Juan Williams. "Finish high school, at least. Wait until your twenties before marrying, and wait until you're married before having children. Once you're in the work force, stay in: take any job, because building on experience will prepare you for a better job." Juan Williams, "Getting Past Katrina," *The New York Times,* 1 September 2006. Williams adds that "[a]ny American who follows that prescription will be at almost no risk of falling into extreme poverty. Statistics show it." Juan Williams, *Enough,* 215.

40. See Chapters 5 and 6.

41. See "'Live' with TAE: Interview with Shelby Steele," *American Enterprise Magazine* (April 2006): 16.

Chapter 3: Racial Disparities and Human Capital Deficits

1. See Stephen Thernstrom and Abigail Thernstrom, *America in Black and White* (New York: Simon & Schuster, 1997).

2. For a detailed account of trends among elementary and high school students, see Derek Neal, "Why Has Black-White Skill Convergence Stopped?" in *The Handbook of Economics of Education,* Vol. 1, Eric A. Hanushek and Finis Welch, eds., (Amsterdam: North-Holland, 2006). See also Derek Neal, "Black-White Labour Market Inequality in the United States," in the *New Palgrave Dictionary of Economics,* 2007; Melanie Phillips and Christopher Jencks, *The Black-White Test Score Gap* (Washington, D.C.: Brookings Institution Press, 1998); Kathryn Neckerman, ed., *Social Inequality* (New York: Russell Sage Foundation Press, 2004), 468–473. For a review of black educational trends and attainment since the 1950s, see Orley Ashenfelter, ed., Special Issue on Brown vs. Board of Education, *American Law and Economics Review* 8 (Summer 2006).

3. Meredith Phillips and Tiffani Chin, "School Inequality: What Do We Know?" in *Social Inequality,* Kathryn Neckerman, ed., (New York: Russell

Sage Foundation Press, 2004), 468–473. See also Alan Krueger, Jesse Rothstein, and Sarah Turner, "Race, Income and College in 25 Years: Evaluating Justice O'Connor's Conjecture," *American Law and Economics Review*
8 (Summer 2006): 285.

4. Neal, "Black-White Labour Market Inequality in the United States." Racial gaps are not confined to scores in reading and math but affect other
important areas of learning. Recent testing of basic science knowledge
in eighth graders nationwide showed black students lagging well behind
whites even within the same school districts. See Diana Jean Schemo,
"Most Students in Big Cities Lag Badly in Basic Science," *The New York
Times,* 16 November 2006, A22.

5. See June Kronholz, "SAT Scores Are Highest Since 1974," *The Wall Street
Journal,* 27 August 2003, A2.

6. Melanie Phillips and Christopher Jencks, *The Black-White Test Score
Gap,* 482.

7. See Krueger, Rothstein, and Turner, "Race, Income and College in 25
Years," documenting the paucity of blacks among top scorers on the
SATs. A black student is about six times more likely than a white student to finish below the fifth percentile in a standardized math test but
only about one-twentieth as likely as a white student to finish above
the ninety-fifth percentile. See Phillips and Jencks, *The Black-White Test
Score Gap,* 158–159, 174–175. Twenty percent of white twelfth-graders were
rated as proficient or advanced on the math section of the 2000 NAEP,
as compared with fewer than five percent of blacks. See Abigail Thernstrom and Stephan Thernstrom, *No Excuses: Closing the Racial Gap in
Learning* (New York: Simon & Schuster, 2003), 16.

8. Phillips and Chin, "School Inequality: What Do We Know?," at 471.

9. For data on test scores by race, education, and income, see sources cited
in notes 6 & 7 *supra*.

10. See Sean Corcoran et al., "The Changing Distribution of Education Fi-
nance, 1972–1997" in *Social Inequality,* ed. Kathryn Neckerman, ed., (New
York: Russell Sage Foundation Press, 1998), 433–465; Phillips and Chin,
"School Inequality: What Do We Know?" 467–519, reviewing data on
school spending and quality from the 1980s and 1990s. On disparities in
school and teacher quality, see also Richard Rothstein, *Class and Schools:
Using Social, Economic, and Educational Reform to Close the Black-White
Achievement Gap* (Washington, D.C.: Economic Policy Institute; New
York: Columbia University Teachers College, 2004), 100–102.

11. See Corcoran et al., "The Changing Distribution of Education Finance, 1972–1997," 433–465; Phillips and Chin, "School Inequality: What Do We Know?," 467–519.

12. Phillips and Chin, "School Inequality: What Do We Know?," 510. See also Corcoran et al., "The Changing Distribution of Education Finance, 1972–1997," 440. The ratio of spending per white student to spending per nonwhite student was 1.02 in 1972, 0.99 in 1982, and 0.97 in 1992.

13. See, e.g., Michael A. Rebell, "Poverty, 'Meaningful' Educational Opportunity, and the Necessary Role of the Courts," *North Carolina Law Review* 85 (June 2007), 1467–1543, at 1479–1482 (reviewing the debate over whether "money matters"); Michael Heise, "Litigated Learning, Law's Limits, and Urban School Reform Challenges," *North Carolina Law Review* 85 (June 2007), 1419–1466, (presenting evidence against the connection between education funding levels and differential achievement); see also id. at 1446–1450 (observing that urban public schools, including those with mostly black students, have been comparatively well-funded in recent decades).

14. Corcoran et al., "The Changing Distribution of Education Finance, 1972–1997," 440–442.

15. Phillips and Chin, "School Inequality: What Do We Know?," 508–510.

16. Lee Jussim and Kent D. Harber, "Teacher Expectations and Self-Fulfilling Prophecies: Knowns and Unknowns, Resolved and Unresolved Controversies," *Personality and Social Psychology Review* 9, 2 (2005): 131–155; see also Lee Jussim, Jacquelynne Eccles, Stephanie Madon, "Social Perception, Social Stereotypes, and Teacher Expectations: Accuracy and the Quest for the Powerful Self-Fulfilling Prophecy" *Advances in Experimental Social Psychology* 28 (1996): 281–288.

17. Jussim and Harber, "Teacher Expectations," 151.

18. *Ibid.*

19. Thomas S. Dee, "Teachers, Race, and Student Achievement in a Randomized Experiment," *Review of Economics and Statistics* 86 (2004): 195. Race matching may actually be detrimental. Minority teachers tend to lag on average in other attributes—such as knowledge of subject matter and measures of cognitive ability—that have been shown to matter to student learning. The tension between race-matching and quality teaching was noted in the 1960s by the sociologist James Coleman. See Linda Seebach, Editorial: "Dissenters Often Offer Better Glimpse of the Truth," *Contra Costa Times* 16 Feb. 1997, A19, stating that "In the 1970s, when sociologist James Coleman was doing research on inequalities of

educational opportunity, he discovered two things: that children's success was strongly affected by their teachers' verbal ability as revealed on standardized tests and that black teachers, many of them trained in segregated schools, did badly on such tests. But the potential implications of the idea that black children might do just as well or better with white teachers were simply unthinkable, and Coleman and his colleagues did not pursue it. Looking back on the episode, Coleman admitted it could be true that 'we aided in the sacrifice of educational opportunity for many children, most of whom were black, to protect the careers of black teachers.'"); Chuck Forrester, Editorial: "Merger Model Could Work with the Right Elements," *Greensboro News and Record* 26 May 1991, B3 stating that "[s]ome years ago the state of North Carolina did a survey to determine how good students are produced. To everyone's surprise class size and per pupil expenditures mattered little, if at all. The quality of teachers was found to be most important. James Coleman had found the same thing in 1964: a direct link between teachers' vocabularies and student achievement.").

20. See Paul R. Sackett et al., "On Interpreting Stereotype Threat as Accounting for African American–White Differences on Cognitive Tests," *American Psychologist* 59, 1 (January 2004): 7–13; Amy L. Wax, "The Threat in the Air," *The Wall Street Journal*, 13 April 2004, A20. For a comprehensive critique of stereotype threat (ST) as an explanation for performance differences by race and gender, see Amy L. Wax, "Stereotype Threat: A Case of Overclaim Syndrome?" in Christina Hoff Sommers, ed., *The Science on Women in Science* (AEI Press, forthcoming April 2009).

21. See Phillips and Chin, "School Inequality: What Do We Know?," 476–479.

22. See Phillips and Chin, "School Inequality: What Do We Know?," 476–479. See also Rothstein, *Class and Schools;* Thomas J. Kane, Jonah Rockoff, and Douglas Staiger, "What Does Certification Tell Us About Teacher Effectiveness? Evidence from New York City," unpublished paper, http://papers.nber.org/papers/w12155.pdf.

23. See Kane, Rockoff, and Staiger. Kane and colleagues claimed to find a link between directly observed teacher quality and student test scores in a study conducted in New York City. They did not look specifically at whether minority children had poorer teachers, however. There is some modest evidence for a relationship between a teacher's cognitive ability (as measured, for example, by IQ tests) and knowledge (as reflected in quality of undergraduate education) and student outcomes. But there

is no consistent, reliable data on whether, in general, minority students have teachers who are less learned or less smart. See, e.g., Rob Greenwald, Larry V. Hedges, and Richard D. Laine, "The Effect of School Resources on Student Achievement," *Review of Educational Research* 66 (1996): 361–396; Linda Darling-Hammond, *Teacher Quality and Student Achievement: A Review of State Policy Evidence* (Seattle: Center for the Study of Teaching and Policy, 1999).

24. Derek Neal, "Black-White Labour Market Inequality in the United States." There is evidence that blacks on average fall short of whites in performance on the job. See Patrick F. McKay and Michael A. McDaniel, "A Re-examination of Black-White Mean Differences in Work Performance: More Data, More Moderators," *J. of Applied Psych.* 91(2006): 538–554 presenting data on "mean racial disparities in work performance." As the authors of this paper note, these observations raise the question of "which aspects of performance underlie these disparities." Id. At 538. Although the answer is complex, the research suggests that differences in work-related skills and abilities account for almost all performance gaps. See also Devah Pager, "The Use of Field Experiments for Studies of Employment Discrimination: Contributions, Critiques, and Directions for the Future," *Annals of the American Academy of Political and Social Sciences* 609 (January 2007): 108 noting numerous "influential studies" showing that "when relevant individual characteristics—in particular, cognitive ability—have been accounted for, racial disparities in wages among young men narrow substantially or disappear"; James Heckman, "Detecting Discrimination," *J. of Econ. Perspectives* 12 (1998): 101 noting that "[m]ost of the disparity in earnings between blacks and whites in the labor market of the 1990s is due to differences in skills they bring to the market, and not to discrimination within the labor market," and describing employment discrimination as "the problem of an earlier era."

25. Derek Neal, "Why Has Black-White Skill Convergence Stopped?": 512–576; see also June O'Neill, "The Role of Human Capital in Earnings Differences Between Black and White Men," *The Journal of Economic Perspectives* 4, 4 (Autumn 1990): 25–45; George Farkas et al. "Cognitive Skill, Skill Demands of Jobs, and Earnings Among Young European American, African American, and Mexican American Workers," *Social Forces* 75 (1997): 913; George Farkas and Keven Vicknair, "Appropriate Tests of Racial Wage Discrimination Require Controls for Cognitive Skill: Comment on Cancio, Evans, and Maume," *American Sociological Review* 61 (August 1996): 557–660; Derek Neal and William Johnson, "The Role

of Pre-market Factors in Black-White Wage Differences," *J. of Political Economy* 104 (1996): 869–895; Barry T. Hirsch and David A. Macpherson, "Wages, Sorting on Skill, and the Racial Composition of Jobs," *Journal of Labor Economics* 22, 1 (2004): 189–210; James Heckman and Dmitri Masterov, "Labor Market Discrimination and Racial Differences in Premarket Factors," in *Handbook of Research on Employment Discrimination, Rights and Realities,* Laura Beth Nielson and Robert Nelson, eds. (New York: Springer, 2005).

26. Derek Neal, "Why Has Black-White Skill Convergence Stopped?"; Richard J. Murnane, John B. Willet, and Frank Levy, "The Growing Importance of Cognitive Skills in Wage Determination," *Review of Economics and Statistics* 77 (1995): 251–266.

27. William R. Johnson and Derek Neal, "Basic Skills and the Black-White Earnings Gap," in *The Black-White Test Score Gap,* Christopher Jencks and Meredith Phillips, eds. (Washington, D.C.: Brookings Institution Press, 1998), 480–497.

28. See Stephen Coate and Glenn C. Loury, "Will Affirmative-Action Policies Eliminate Negative Stereotypes?" *American Economic Review* 83 (1993): 1220–1240.

29. Johnson and Neal, "Basic Skills and the Black-White Earnings Gap," 495.

30. Devah Pager and Lincoln Quillian, "Walking the Talk? What Employers Say Versus What They Do," *American Sociological Review* 70 (2005): 355–380. See also Devah Pager, *Marked: Race, Crime, and Finding Work in an Era of Mass Incarceration* (Chicago: University of Chicago Press, 2007).

31. Marianne Bertrand and Sendhil Mullainathan, "Are Emily and Greg More Employable Than Lakisha and Jamal? A Field Experiment on Labor Market Discrimination," *The American Economic Review* 94, 4 (September 2004): 991–1013.

32. P. A. Riach and J. Rich, "Field Experiments of Discrimination in the Market Place," *The Economic Journal* 112 (November 2002): F480–F518.

33. On rational discrimination, see Richard Epstein, *Forbidden Grounds: The Case Against Employment Discrimination Laws* (Cambridge: Harvard University Press, 1992). See also Gary Becker, *The Economics of Discrimination* (Chicago: University of Chicago Press, 1971).

34. See Sam Dillon, "Schools Slow in Closing Gaps Between Races," *The New York Times,* 20 November 2006, A1, noting that "African American and Hispanic students in high school can read and do arithmetic at only the average level of whites in junior high school"; Rene Sanchez, "Colleges Compete for Minority Students by Helping Them Achieve," *The*

Washington Post, 28 Dec. 1996, A1, explaining that "In California, for example, only 5 percent of black graduates from public schools in the state, and only 4 percent of Hispanic graduates, now meet the university system's admissions standards. That compares with 13 percent of whites."

35. See notes 51 and 53, this chapter, infra.

36. See Joleyn Kirschenman and Kathryn Neckerman, "We'd Love to Hire Them, But. . ." in *The Urban Underclass,* Christopher Jencks and Paul E. Peterson, eds. (Washington, D.C.: The Brookings Institution, 1992); Elijah Anderson, *Code of the Streets: Decency, Violence, and the Moral Life of the Inner City* (New York: Norton, 1999); Tanya Mohn, "Sometimes the Right Approach Is Putting the Best Face Forward," *New York Times,* 7 May 2006, sec. 10, p. 1 (noting that some inner-city black men develop the habit of wearing a "game face," or menacing expression, that employers find intimidating).

37. Roland G. Fryer, Jr. and Steven D. Levitt, "The Causes and Consequences of Distinctively Black Names" *The Quarterly Journal of Economics* 119, 3 (August 2004): 767–805, explaining negative employer responses to black names as a reaction to those names' association with lower social class, which is in turn linked to lower job productivity.

38. David T. Ellwood and Jonathan Crane, "Family Change Among Black Americans: What Do We Know?" *Journal of Economic Perspectives* 4, 4 (Autumn 1990): 65. For a comprehensive overview of the most recent data on family structure by race and class, see U.S. Census Bureau, Current Population Survey (CPS) Reports, *America's Families and Living Arrangements: 2008,* at http://www. census.gov/population/www/socdemo/hh-fam .html.

39. David T. Ellwood and Christopher Jencks, "The Uneven Spread of Single-Parent Families: What Do We Know? Where Do We Look for Answers?" in *Social Inequality,* Kathryn M. Neckerman, ed. (New York: Russell Sage Foundation, 2004), 3–77; David T. Ellwood and Christopher Jencks, "The Spread of Single-Parent Families in the United States Since 1960," in Daniel P. Moynihan, Timothy M. Smeeding, and Lee Rainwater, eds., *The Future of the Family* (New York: Russell Sage Foundation, 2004), 25–65; Sara McLanahan, "Diverging Destinies: How Children Are Faring Under the Second Demographic Transition," *Demography* 41, 4 (November 2004); 607–627. For a review of recent trends in family structure and possible explanations, see Amy L. Wax, "Engines of Inequality: Class, Race, and Family Structure," *Family Law Quarterly* (Fall 2007), 567–599.

40. In 1960, 80 percent of black women and 66 percent of black men aged

20–34 were married at least once. By 1990, those figures had declined to 46 percent and 38 percent, respectively. See Robert G. Wood, "Marriage Rates and Marriageable Men: A Test of the Wilson Hypothesis," *Journal of Human Resources* 30 (1995): 163.

41. See Cassandra Logan et al., *Men Who Father Children with More Than One Woman: A Contemporary Portrait of Multiple Partner Fertility* (Washington, D.C.: Childtrends Publication #2006-10, 2006), showing that black men are twice as likely as white men to have children by more than one woman. See also Maria Cancian and Daniel R. Meyer, "The Economic Circumstances of Fathers with Children on W-2," *FOCUS* 22 (Summer 2002), 19, 21–23; Karen B. Guzzo and Frank F. Furstenberg, Jr., "Multi-partnered Fertility Among American Men," *Demography* 44 (August 2007), 583–601 (presenting data that black men are significantly more likely than others to have children by more than one woman). For an overview of developments within the black family, see Kay S. Hymowitz, *Marriage and Caste in America* (Chicago: Ivan R. Dee, 2006).

42. See Sara McLanahan, "Diverging Destinies: How Children Are Faring Under the Second Demographic Transition," *Demography* 41, 4 (November 2004): 607–626, noting that the out-of-wedlock childbearing rate to white college-educated women in the 1990s remained well under 5 percent. See also Steven P. Martin, "Growing Evidence for a 'Divorce Divide'? Education and Marital Dissolution Rates in the U.S. Since the 1970s," *Demographic Research* 15 (2006): 537–560, noting declining divorce rates among well-educated whites.

43. See Kristin Anderson Moore et al., "Marriage from a Child's Perspective: How Does Family Structure Affect Children?" *Childtrends Research Brief* (2002); Wendy Sigle-Rushton and Sara McLanahan, "Father Absence and Child Well-Being: A Critical Review," in *The Future of the Family,* Daniel Patrick Moynihan et al., eds. (New York: Russell Sage Foundation, 2004), 116–155; Abigail Thernstrom and Stephan Thernstrom, *No Excuses: Closing the Racial Gap in Learning* (New York: Simon & Schuster, 2003), 132; McLanahan, "Diverging Destinies," 607–627.

44. McLanahan, "Diverging Destinies," 607–627.

45. See Kathryn Edin and Maria Kefalas, *Promises I Can Keep: Why Poor Women Put Motherhood Before Marriage* (Berkeley: University of California Press, 2005), 215, noting that *"living apart from either biological parent at any point during childhood is what seems to hurt children"* (emphasis in original). See also Donna K. Ginther and Robert A. Pollak, "Family Structure and Children's Educational Outcomes: Blended Families, Stylized Facts, and

Descriptive Regressions," *Demography* 41 (November 2004): 671–696; Sandra Hofferth, "Residential Father Family Type and Child Well-Being: Investment Versus Selection," *Demography* 43 (Feb. 2006): 53–77. For a recent summary of the social science evidence on family structure and child well-being to date, see Kristin Anderson Moore et al., "Marriage from a Child's Perspective: How Does Family Structure Affect Children and What Can We Do About It?" *Child Trends Research Brief* (June 2002).

46. Patricia Schnitzer and Bernard Ewigman, "Child Deaths Resulting from Inflicted Injuries: Household Risk Factors and Perpetrator Characteristics," *Pediatrics* 116 (November 2005): e687–e689.

47. See Derek Neal, "Why has Black-White Skill Convergence Stopped?" 512–576.

48. See Valerie E. Lee and David T. Burkam, *Inequality at the Starting Gate: Social Background Differences in Achievement as Children Begin School* (Washington, D.C.: Economic Policy Institute, 2002); Petra Todd, "The Production of Cognitive Achievement in Children: Home, School and Racial Test Score Gaps," unpublished ms., at http://www.econ.brown.edu/econ/events/revpaper.pdf

49. See Valerie E. Lee and David T. Burkam, *Inequality at the Starting Gate*.

50. *Ibid.*

51. For noncognitive attributes as predictors of subsequent outcomes on a broad range of social indicators, see James J. Heckman, Jora Stixrud, and Sergio Urzua, "The Effect of Cognitive and Noncognitive Abilities on Labor Market Outcomes and Social Behavior," *Journal of Labor Economics* 24, 3 (2006): 411–482; James Heckman and Yona Rubinstein, "The Importance of Noncognitive Skills: Lessons from the GED Testing Program," *American Economic Review* 91 (2001): 145–149; See also Angela Lee Duckworth, *Intelligence Is Not Enough: Non-IQ Predictors of Achievement* (unpublished doctoral dissertation, chapter 3, University of Pennsylvania); Angela L. Duckworth, Christopher Peterson, Michael D. Matthews and Dennis R. Kelly, "Grit: Perseverance and Passion for Long-Term Goals," *Journal of Personality and Social Psychology* 92 (2007): 1087–1101.

52. Richard Rothstein, *Class and Schools,* 100–102.

53. See David Autor and David Scarborough, "Will Job Testing Harm Minority Workers?" *Quarterly Journal of Economics* 123, 1 (Feb. 2008): 219–77 presenting data that reveal group differences on personality tests of job-related attributes like agreeableness and conscientiousness. See also Lewis R. Goldberg et al., "Demographic Variables and Personality: The Effects of Gender, Age, Education, and Ethnic/Racial Status

on Self-Descriptions of Personality Attributes," *Personality and Individual Differences* 24, 3 (1998): 393–403, finding some average personality differences between whites, blacks, and Hispanics in a large national sample.

54. See James J. Heckman and Alan B. Krueger, *Inequality in America: What Role for Human Capital Policies?* (Cambridge: MIT Press, 2003).

55. See Roland G. Fryer and Steven D. Levitt, "The Black-White Test Score Gap Through Third Grade," *American Law and Economics Review* 8 (Summer 2006): 249–281.

56. See Judith Harris, *The Nurture Assumption: Why Children Turn Out the Way They Do* (New York: Free Press, 1998). See also Richard D. Kahlenberg, *The Remedy: Race, Class, and Affirmative Action* (New York: Basic Books, 1996); Richard D. Kahlenberg, *All Together Now: Creating Middle-Class Schools Through Public Choice* (Washington, D.C.: Brookings Institution Press, 2001) noting the importance of peer influence in schools.

57. See John U. Ogbu, *Black American Students in an Affluent Suburb: A Study of Academic Disengagement* (Mahwah, N.J.: Lawrence Erlbaum Associates, 2003) describing the "empty vessel" outlook on learning.

58. See Myron Lieberman, *The Educational Morass: Overcoming the Stalemate in American Education* (Lanham, Maryland: Rowman & Littlefield Education, 2007), at 4 ("The differences between the effects of parents who encourage reading, emphasize the importance of education, . . . and foster good work habits (and many others conducive to high achievement) . . . and those parents who do none of these things have never been substantially eliminated by any system of education."). Richard Kahlenberg in *All Together Now* argues that controlling the socioeconomic mix of students can cause underperforming children to improve through the beneficial influence of more privileged peers. In addition to being virtually impossible to achieve, such forced social class mixing has never been shown to produce the promised results. In addition, given the vagaries of peer dynamics, there is no guarantee that influence will run in the desired direction or that desirable habits will triumph. Bad habits can defeat good ones as easily as the good can uplift the bad.

59. Two books looking at different groups of students within the same schools are John U. Ogbu, *Black American Students in an Affluent Suburb: A Study of Academic Disengagement* (Mahwah, N.J.: Lawrence Erlbaum Associates, 2003) and Laurence Steinberg, *Beyond the Classroom: Why School Reform Has Failed and What Parents Need to Do* (New York: Simon & Schuster, 1996). For strong evidence that achievement gaps between

blacks and whites cannot be attributed to differences in school quality, see Roland G. Fryer and Steven D. Levitt, "The Black-White Test Score Gap Through Third Grade," *American Law and Economics Review* 8 (Summer 2006): 271. The authors conclude that most of the differences in test scores between blacks and whites in their sample of over 20,000 students in 1000 schools remain even after controlling for school quality. They note that nearly all the observed growth in black-white disparities between first and third grade "is within rather than across schools."

60. The extent to which an aversion to "acting white" is a significant factor in depressing black student achievement remains controversial. See Roland G. Fryer, Jr. and Paul Torelli, "An Empirical Analysis of 'Acting White'" (Working Paper, May 1, 2005); Roland G. Fryer, "Acting White," *Education Next* (Winter 2006): 53–59. The link between students' and families' attitudes toward education and student achievement by race is not straightforward. Although blacks seem to embrace the prevalent view that education is important to success, those beliefs don't seem consistently to translate into actual achievement. See, e.g., Harold W. Stevenson, Chuansheng Chen, and David H. Uttal, "Belief and Achievement: A Study of Black, White, and Hispanic Children," 61 *Child Development* (April 1990): 508–523. There is some evidence that specific beliefs about the relationship between an individual's own educational effort and his or her personal life chances, rather than more abstract beliefs about the value of education generally, are more predictive of educational outcomes. At least one study purports to show that blacks differ significantly from whites in concrete attitudes to education. See Roslyn Mickelson, "The Attitude–Achievement Paradox among Black Adolescents," 63 *Sociology of Education* (Jan. 1990): 44–61.

61. See James J. Heckman and Alan B. Krueger, *Inequality in America: What Role for Human Capital Policies?* (Cambridge: MIT Press, 2003). Fryer and Levitt, using the Early Childhood Longitudinal Study, find that black students in the fall of their kindergarten year score about 0.64 standard deviations behind whites on the math portion of a standardized test and 0.40 standard deviations behind whites in reading, "The Black-White Test Score Gap Through Third Grade." Within the CNLSY cohort (Children of the National Longitudinal Survey of Youth), Jencks and Phillips observe that black five- and six-year-olds between 1986 and 1992 (when the racial gap generally was at its narrowest) scored about one standard deviation behind whites on a standardized vocabulary test. See Melanie

Phillips and Christopher Jencks, *The Black-White Test Score Gap* (Washington, D.C.: Brookings Institution Press, 1998), 108.

62. Fryer and Levitt find black kindergarteners falling behind whites by an additional 0.09 standard deviation in math, and 0.128 standard deviation in reading, by spring of first grade. By contrast, the Hispanic-white gap shrinks between the beginning of kindergarten and the end of first grade. See "The Black-White Test Score Gap through Third Grade."

63. See James Coleman et al., *Equality of Educational Opportunity* (Washington, D.C.: U.S. Department of Health, Education, and Welfare, Office of Education, 1966).

64. See Rothstein, *Class and Schools,* 100–102.

65. Pedro Carneiro, James J. Heckman, and Dimitriy V. Masterov, "Labor Market Discrimination and Racial Differences in Premarket Factors," *J. of Law and Economics* 48 (April 2005): 1–39; Flavio Cunha, James J. Heckman, Lance Lochner, and Dimitriy V. Masterov, "Interpreting the Evidence on Life Cycle Skill Formation," *Handbook of the Economics of Education,* Vol. 1 (2005): 698–812; James J. Heckman and Alan B. Krueger, *Inequality in America: What Role for Human Capital Policies?* (Cambridge: MIT Press, 2003). See also Sarah E. Turner, "Going to College and Finishing College—Explaining Different Educational Outcomes," in *College Choices: The Economics of Where to Go, When to Go, and How to Pay for It,* Caroline Hoxby, ed. (Chicago: The University of Chicago Press, 2006), 47, suggesting that "factors beyond financial constraints, including academic achievement, are the factors limiting college enrollment and college attainment for the marginal low-income student."

66. Meredith Phillips and Tiffani Chin, "School Inequality: What Do We Know?" in *Social Inequality,* Kathryn Neckerman, ed. (New York: Russell Sage Foundation Press, 2004), 471.

67. Pedro Carneiro and James J. Heckman, "Human Capital Policy" in *Inequality in America: What Role for Human Capital Policies?* James J. Heckman and Alan B. Krueger, eds. (Cambridge: MIT Press, 2002), 101.

68. Editorial, "Tough Lesson," *Winston-Salem Journal,* 28 Jan. 2007, sec. A p. 14 describing Democratic college aid proposals; see also Brian Fiel, "No Funding Left Behind," *The National Journal,* 9 Sept. 2006, sec. Education, describing proposals for college aid.

69. Rothstein, *Class and Schools,* 100–102.

70. See Leslie J. Calman and Linda Tarr-Whelan, *Early Childhood Education for All: A Wise Investment* (New York: Legal Momentum, April 2005).

71. See *ibid.* See also James J. Heckman and Alan B. Krueger, *Inequality in America: What Role for Human Capital Policies?* (Cambridge: MIT Press, 2003); Lawrence J. Schweinhart, "The High/Scope Perry Preschool Study Through Age 40: Summary, Conclusions, and Frequently Asked Questions" (Ypsilanti, Mich.: High/Scope Educational Research Foundation, November 2004).

72. See Carneiro and Heckman, "Human Capital Policy," 78–239; Rothstein, *Class and Schools,* 99–102.

73. See Schweinhart, "The High/Scope Perry Preschool Study"; Calman and Tarr-Whelan, *Early Childhood Education for All.* On economic impacts, see James Heckman, "Catch 'Em Young," *The Wall Street Journal,* 10 January 2006, A14.

74. See Charles Murray and Richard Herrnstein, *The Bell Curve* (New York: Free Press, 1994).

75. Some twin cross-adoption studies suggest that the gap in average IQ between blacks and whites in part reflects genetic differences. See Sandra Scarr, Richard Weinberg, and Irwin Waldman, "IQ Correlations in Transracial Adoptive Families," *Intelligence* 17 (1993): 541–555. Other studies suggest that, while genes contribute something to IQ for children in average or superior homes, environmental factors overwhelm genetics for those, like inner-city black children, who grow up in deprived environments. See Eric Turkheimer et al., "Socioeconomic Status Modifies Heritability of IQ in Young Children," *Psychological Science* 14 (November 2003): 623. See also James R. Flynn, "IQ Gains over Time: Toward Finding the Causes," in *The Rising Curve: Long-Term Gains in IQ and Related Measures,* Ulric Neisser, ed. (Washington: American Psychological Association, 1998), 25–66; James R. Flynn, "IQ Trends over Time: Intelligence, Race, and Meritocracy," in *Meritocracy and Economic Inequality,* Kenneth Arrow, Samuel Bowles, and Steven N. Durlauf, eds. (Princeton: Princeton University Press, 2000), 35–60.

76. See Charles Murray, "Intelligence in the Classroom," *The Wall Street Journal,* January 16, 2007, at A21.

77. See Valerie E. Lee and David T. Burkam, *Inequality at the Starting Gate: Social Background Differences in Achievement as Children Begin School* (Washington, D.C.: Economic Policy Institute, 2002); David Armor, *Maximizing Intelligence* (New Brunswick: Transaction Publishers, 2003); David Armor, "*Brown* and Black-White Achievement," *Academic Questions* 19 2 (2006): 40–53; Betty Hart and Todd R. Risley, *Meaningful Differences in the Everyday Experiences of Young American Children* (Baltimore: Paul H. Brooks,

1995); Roland G. Fryer and Steven D. Levitt, "The Black-White Test Score Gap Through Third Grade," *American Law and Economics Review* 8 (Summer 2006): 249–281. But see Judith Harris, *The Nurture Assumption: Why Children Turn Out the Way They Do* (New York: Free Press, 1998), suggesting that the importance of home environment to development is exaggerated, but conceding the potential influence of group culture.

78. See Judith Harris, *The Nurture Assumption,* which questions whether parental behavior has much influence on children's personalities but acknowledges that early childhood experiences may affect IQ. See also David Armor, *Maximizing Intelligence.*

79. William A. Sampson, *Black Student Achievement: How Much Do Family and School Really Matter?* (Lanham, Maryland: The Scarecrow Press, 2002), 200.

80. See Chapter 5.

81. Derek Neal and William Johnson, "The Role of Pre-Market Factors in Black-White Wage Differences," *J. of Political Economy* 104 (1996): 869–895; Neal, "Why has Black-White Skill Convergence Stopped?" 512–576.

82. For a review of this literature, see, e.g., Sam Bagenstos, "The Structural Turn and the Limits of Anti-discrimination Law," *California L. Review* 94 (January 2006): 1–48. See also Susan Sturm, "Second Generation Employment Discrimination: A Structural Approach," *Columbia Law Review* 101 (2001): 458; Julie Chi-hye Suk, "Anti-discrimination Law in the Administrative State," 2006 *Univ. Of Illinois Law Review* 405–473.

83. See Julie Chi-hye Suk, "Anti-discrimination Law in the Administrative State," 417.

84. *Ibid.*

85. See Anthony G. Greenwald and Linda Hamilton Krieger, "Implicit Bias: Scientific Foundations," *California Law Review* 94 (July 2006): 945–967; Jerry Kang, "Trojan Horses of Race," *Harv. L. Rev.* 118 (2005): 1491, 1537.

86. See Sam Bagenstos, "The Structural Turn and the Limits of Anti-discrimination Law"; Amy L. Wax, "Discrimination as Accident," *Indiana Law J.* 47 (Fall 1999): 1129.

87. See Hal R. Arkes and Phillip E. Tetlock, "Attributions of Implicit Prejudice, or "Would Jesse Jackson 'Fail' the Implicit Association Test?," *Psychological Inquiry* 15 (2004): 257–278.

88. See Christine Jolls, "Anti-Discrimination Law's Effects on Implicit Bias," in *Behavioral Analyses of Workplace Discrimination: A Volume in Honor of David Charny* (forthcoming), 16 (stating that "evidence linking measures of implicit bias to observed behavior does not establish any con-

nection between such measures and the types of decisions that anti-discrimination law polices. . . . [T]he social science evidence has not yet established that these kinds of decisions are in fact driven by implicit bias as measured by the IAT and similar tests.") See also R. Richard Banks, Jennifer Eberhardt, and Lee Ross, "Discrimination and Implicit Bias in a Racially Unequal Society," *California L. Rev.* 94: 1169–1190, 1187 ("Thus far, however, there is little evidence that Race IAT scores correlate with discrimination against African Americans."); Hart M. Blanton, James Jaccard, Jonathan Klick, Barbara Mellers, Gregory Mitchell, and Philip E. Tetlock, "Strong Claims and Weak Evidence: Reassessing the Predictive Validity of the IAT," *Journal of Applied Psychology* 94 (forthcoming 2009) (finding no evidence that IAT scores predict discriminatory behavior). For a comprehensive review and critique of the literature on unconscious bias, and a discussion of the difficulty of separating the influence of unconscious bias from supply side factors, see Amy L. Wax, "The Discriminating Mind: Define It, Prove It," *Connecticut Law Review* 40 (2008): 979.

89. See Michael I. Norton et al., "Casuistry and Social Category Bias," *J. of Personality and Social Psychology* 87 (2004): 817, noting evidence that individuating information can override stereotyping; Eliot R. Smith, et al., "Familiarity Can Increase Stereotyping," *J. of Exp. Soc. Psychology* 42 (2006): 471–478, observing that familiarity with particular individuals from a social group can have variable effects on laboratory measures of bias; Hart M. Blanton, James Jaccard, Jonathan Klick, Barbara Mellers, Gregory Mitchell, and Philip E. Tetlock, "Strong Claims and Weak Evidence: Reassessing the Predictive Validity of the IAT,"(forthcoming in *Journal of Applied Psychology*), finding that some studies link high IAT bias with pro-black behavior.

90. See, e.g., James Heckman, Robert LaLonde, and Jeffrey Smith, "The Economics and Econometrics of Active Labor Market Policies," in *The Handbook of Labor Economics,* Vol. 3A, Orley Ashenfelter and David Card, eds. (Amsterdam: North-Holland, 1999): 1865–2097; David B. Muhlhausen, "Do Jobs Programs Work?: A Review Article," *J. of Labor Research* 26 (Spring 2005): 299.

91. See James Heckman, Robert LaLonde, and Jeffrey Smith, "The Economics and Econometrics of Active Labor Market Policies," 2080.

92. See, e.g., Stephen J. Ceci and Paul B. Papierno, "The Rhetoric and Reality of Gap Closing: When the 'Have-Nots' Gain but the 'Haves' Gain Even More," *American Psychologist* 60, no. 2 (February–March 2005): 149–160.

93. See discussion in Chapter 6.

94. See Cass Sunstein, "Why Markets Don't Stop Discrimination," *Soc. Phil. & Policy Review* 8 (Spring 1991): 22–37; Stewart Schwab, "Is Statistical Discrimination Efficient," *American Econ. Rev.* 76 (1986): 228.

95. See Lawrence Mead, *The New Politics of Poverty: The Nonworking Poor in America* (New York: Basic Books, 1993), 83.

96. See, e.g., Joleyn Kirschenman and Kathryn Neckerman, "'We'd Really Love to Hire Them, But. . . .'," 203–232. But see Richard Rothstein, *Class and Schools*, 99–102 (reviewing evidence for racial differences in children's socialization).

97. For a description of the *Strive* program, see Kay Hymowitz, "At Last: A Job Program That Works," *City Journal* (Winter 1997); see also Tanya Mohn, "Sometimes the Right Approach Is Putting the Best Face Forward," *The New York Times,* 7 May 2006, sec. 10, p. 1.

98. See Ellwood and Jencks, "The Spread of Single-Parent Families in the United States Since 1960"; M. Belinda Tucker and Claudia Mitchell-Kernan, eds., *The Decline in Marriage Among African Americans: Causes, Consequences, and Policy Implications* (New York: Russell Sage Foundation, 1995); Heather Koball, "Have African American Men become Less Committed to Marriage? Explaining the Twentieth Century Racial Cross-Over in Men's Marriage Timing," *Demography,* 35, 2 (May 1998): 251–258.

99. Ellwood and Jencks, "The Uneven Spread of Single-Parent Families," 35. As summarized in one comprehensive review, "racial differences in mate availability account for a relatively small share of existing racial differences in marriage." Daniel T. Lichter, et al. "Race and the Retreat from Marriage: A Shortage of Marriageable Men?" *American Sociological Review* 57 (1992): 794.

100. See Lynn White and Stacy J. Rogers, "Economic Circumstances and Family Outcomes: A Review of the 1990s," *Journal of Marriage and the Family* 62 (2000): 1040–1041; Jessie M. Tzeng and Robert D. Mare, "Labor Market and Socioeconomic Effects on Marital Stability," *Social Science Research* 24 (1995): 329. See also Robert D. Mare and Christopher Winship, "Socio-Economic Change and the Decline of Marriage for Blacks and Whites," in *The Urban Underclass,* Christopher Jencks and Paul E. Peterson, eds. (Washington, D.C.: The Brookings Institution, 1991), 174–202; Daniel T. Lichter et al., "Local Marriage Markets and the Marital Behavior of Black and White Women," *American J. of Sociology* 96 (1991): 843–867; Daniel Lichter et al., "Race and the Retreat from Marriage: A

Shortage of Marriageable Men?" *American Sociological Review* 57 (1992): 781–799; David T. Ellwood and Jonathan Crane, "Family Change Among Black Americans: What Do We Know?" *Journal of Economic Perspectives* 4, 4 (Autumn 1990): 65; Robert Schoen and James R. Kluegel, "The Widening Gap in Black and White Marriage Rates: The Impact of Population Composition and Differential Marriage Propensities," *American Sociological Review* 53 (1988): 895.

101. See Edin and Kefalas, *Promises I Can Keep.*

102. Robert I. Lerman, "How Do Marriage, Cohabitation, and Single Parenthood Affect the Material Hardships of Families with Children?" (Prepared for the U.S. Department of Health and Human Services' Office, July 2002); Robert Lerman, "Effects of Marriage on Family Economic Well-Being" (Prepared for the Urban Institute and American University, July 2002).

103. See Sanders Korenman and David Neumark, "Does Marriage Really Make Men More Productive," *J. Of Human Resources* 26 (1990): 282–307; Avner Ahituv and Robert I. Lerman, "How Do Marital Status, Wage Rates, and Work Commitment Interact?" *Urban Institute: IZA DP No.* 1688 (July 2005).

104. See Robert G. Wood, "Marriage Rates and Marriageable Men: A Test of the Wilson Hypothesis," *Journal of Human Resources* 30 (1995): 163.

105. See Kristen Harknett and Sara S. McLanahan, "Racial and Ethnic Differences in Marriage After the Birth of a Child," *American Sociological Review* 69 (2004): 790–811; see also Joshua R. Goldstein and Kristin S. Harknett, "Parenting Across Racial and Class Lines: Assortative Mating Patterns of New Parents Who Are Married, Cohabitating, Dating or No Longer Romantically Involved," *Social Forces* 85, no. 1 (September 2006): 121–143, finding that race predicts willingness to marry, with new parents less likely to marry if one parent is black, even after controlling for other factors.

106. Kristin Harknett and Sara S. McLanahan, "Racial and Ethnic Differences in Marriage After the Birth of a Child." *American Sociological Review* 69 (2004): 790–811; Kristin Harknett and Sara McLanahan, "Mate Availability and the Quality of Non-marital Childbearing Partners," unpublished ms. on file with author (suggesting that marriage markets favorable to men are associated with less harmonious relationships).

107. See Orlando Patterson, *Rituals of Blood: Consequences of Slavery in Two American Centuries* (Washington, D.C.: Civitas/CounterPoint, 1998); Nathan E. Fosse, *Sex, Self-Worth and the Inner City: Procreation and 'Boundary*

Work' Among the Truly Disadvantaged (Unpublished doctoral dissertation, draft, Harvard University, observing the most inner city men in the author's research sample maintain multiple sexual relationships simultaneously); Christopher R. Browning and Lori A. Burrington, "Racial Differences in Sexual and Fertility Attitudes in an Urban Setting," *J. of Marriage and Family* 68 (February 2006): 236–251. See also "Baby Fathers and American Family Formation: Low-Income, Never Married Parents in Louisiana before Katrina," Ronald Mincy and Hillard Pouncy, eds., *An Essay in the Future of the Black Family Series,* Center for Marriage and Families at the Institute for American Values (New York, 2007) 5, 19, 21 (noting that within a Louisiana sample of poor parents that is more than 80% black, 69% of mothers and 65% of fathers agreed that most partners "can't be trusted to be faithful" in a relationship; and reporting that "many men indicated that they did not intend to be faithful to their partner and still considered themselves players in the dating game.")

108. Kathryn Edin and Maria Kefalas, *Promises I Can Keep,* Chapter 2.

109. See sources cited in note 41 supra.

110. See Korenman and Neumark, "Does Marriage Really Make Men More Productive," 282–307; Ahituv and Lerman, "How Do Marital Status, Wage Rates, and Work Commitment Interact?".

111. Kristin Harknett and Sara McLanahan, "Racial and Ethnic Differences in Marriage After the Birth of a Child," 803.

112. Kristin Harknett and Sara McLanahan, "Racial and Ethnic Differences in Marriage after the Birth of a Child," 790.

113. *Ibid.*, 802 explaining racial and ethnic differences. See also Joshua R. Goldstein and Kristin S. Harknett, "Parenting Across Racial and Class Lines: Assortative Mating Patterns of New Parents Who Are Married, Cohabitating, Dating or No Longer Romantically Involved."

114. See Charles Murray, *Losing Ground: American Social Policy, 1950–1980* (New York: Basic Books, 1984); Myron Magnet, *The Dream and the Nightmare: The Sixties' Legacy to the Underclass* (San Francisco: Encounter Books, 2000; New York: Morrow, 1993).

115. Nor can government do much about the recent fragmentation of lower-class families in general, which exacerbates social and economic inequality among Hispanics and whites. See McLanahan, "Diverging Destinies," 607–627.

116. Roger Clegg, "Books in Brief," review of Tavis Smiley, ed., *The Covenant with Black America, The Weekly Standard,* 15 May 2006, 43.

117. *Ibid.*

118. See Hilary Hoynes et al., "Poverty in America: Trends and Explanations," *J. of Economic Perspectives* 20 (Winter 2006), 47–68; Amy L. Wax, "Engines of Inequality: Race, Class, and Family Structure," *Family Law Quarterly* 41 (Fall 2007): 567.

119. See Sara McLanahan, "Diverging Destinies," 607–627; see also Kay Hymowitz, *Marriage and Caste in America* (Chicago: Ivan R. Dee, 2006).

120. See Stephanie Coontz, *The Way We Never Were: American Families and the Nostalgia Trap* (New York: Basic Books, 1992); see also Frank Furstenberg, "Can Marriage Be Saved," *Dissent* (Summer 2005).

121. See Susan Mayer, *What Money Can't Buy: Family Income and Children's Life Chances* (Cambridge: Harvard University Press, 1997).

122. Ian Ayres et al., "Market Power and Inequality: A Competitive Conduct Standard for Assessing When Disparate Impacts are Unjustified," *California Law Review* 95 (2007): 669; see also Ian Ayres, "Fair Driving: Gender and Race Discrimination in Retail Car Negotiations," *Harvard Law Review* 104 (February 1991): 817.

123. Ian Ayres, "Fair Driving," 835.

124. *Ibid.*, 841.

125. See Leonard Pitts Jr., "Failing to Recognize the Effects of Racism," *The Philadelphia Inquirer,* 22 May 2006, A15; Coramae Richey Mann, *Unequal Justice* (Bloomington: Indiana University Press, 1993).

126. See Steven R. Donziger, ed., *The Real War on Crime: The Report of the National Criminal Justice Commission* (New York: Harper Perennial, 1996), 107. "Relative to population size, about five times as many African Americans as whites get arrested for the serious index crimes of murder, rape, robbery, and aggravated assault. About three times as many . . . get arrested for less serious crimes."); See also Michael Tonry, *Malign Neglect—Race, Crime, and Punishment in America* (New York: Oxford University Press, 1995), 49. "In 1991, for example, blacks made up a bit under 13 percent of the general population, but 44.8 percent of those arrested for violent felonies and nearly 50 percent of those in prison on an average day."

127. Tonry, *Malign Neglect,* 50.

128. *Ibid.*, 71. See also Bruce Western, *Punishment and Inequality in America* (New York: Russell Sage, 2006), 49–50, conceding that disadvantaged and poor black men are "greatly involved" in "violence and other crime."

129. Tonry, *Malign Neglect,* 79.

130. See *And Justice for Some,* report from Building Blocks for Youth (2000), available at www.buildingblocksforyouth.org. See also Olatunde C. A.

Johnson, "Disparity Rules," *Columbia Law Review* 107 (2007): 374; Amy L. Wax, "The Discriminating Mind: Define It, Prove It," *Connecticut Law Review* 40 (2008): 988–992 discussing factors that might lead to racial differences in the disposition of juvenile offenders.

131. See Fox Butterfield, "Race Bias Cited Throughout Juvenile Justice System," *San Francisco Chronicle,* 26 April 2000, A1.

132. See Johnson, "Disparity Rules," 405, noting that group differences in family structure, supervision of youth, and cooperation with officials may help explain why black juvenile offenders are more likely to be confined to institutions than white youth.

133. See Western, *Punishment and Inequality in America.*

134. See Michael Tonry, *Thinking About Crime—Sense and Sensibility in American Penal Culture* (New York: Oxford University Press, 2004), 223–226, noting that reducing the penalties for violent offenses would decrease the number of blacks in jail but also could undermine deterrence and increase black victimization rates.

135. Western, *Punishment and Inequality in America.*

Chapter 4: The Psychology of Victimization

1. See Bob Herbert, "A Voice Raised in Chicago," *New York Times,* July 17, 2007.

2. Cornel West, *Race Matters* (Boston: Beacon Press, 1993), 18–19, 59. Consider the 2006 Father's Day message from Senator Evan Bayh and then-Senator Barack Obama. In that message, the lawmakers urge that we "pause to remember the millions of American children living without a father," and remind ourselves of the disadvantages those children suffer. They assert that solving this problem first requires a "change in attitude" to acknowledge that "government can't legislate responsibility." They then go on to link this call for attitude change with recommendations for a range of policies designed to "make it easier for those who make the courageous choice." They propose a federal "Responsible Fatherhood and Healthy Families Act," which includes funding for job training, reductions in marriage tax penalties, expansion of the earned income tax credit, and stricter child support enforcement. See Evan Bayh and Barack Obama, "Real Fathers Don't Abandon Their Children: Legislation Would Help Those Trying To Do the Right Thing and Punish Those Who Didn't," *Philadelphia Inquirer,* 18 June 2006, C07.

Although none of these proposals is objectionable, there is no basis for thinking that any would have more than a negligible impact on men's behavior.

3. Daryl Michael Scott, *Social Policy and the Image of the Damaged Black Psyche, 1880–1996* (Chapel Hill: The University of North Carolina Press, 1997).

4. Herbert M. Lefcourt, "Internal Versus External Control of Reinforcement: A Review," *Psychological Bulletin* 65 (1966): 206–220. A related literature looks at "explanatory style." For a review, see Christopher Peterson, "The Future of Optimism," *American Psychologist* 55 (January 2000): 44–55. See also Martin E. P. Seligman, *Learned Optimism* (New York: Pocket Books, 1990).

5. See Rachel Dunifon and Greg J. Duncan, "Long-Run Effects of Motivation on Labor-Market Success," *Social Psychology Quarterly* 61, 1 (1998): 46, using data from the Panel Study of Income Dynamics to find that "individuals professing both an orientation towards challenge and a belief that their own actions are effective earn considerably higher wages."

6. Naomi Fejgin, "Factors Contributing to the Academic Excellence of American Jewish and Asian Students," *Sociology of Education* 68 (Jan. 1995): 18–30. See also Mildred R. Buck and Harvey R. Austrin, "Factors Related to School Achievement in an Economically Disadvantaged Group," *Child Development* 42 (Dec. 1971): 1817.

7. See, for example, Donald E. Carter and James A. Walsh, "Father Absence and the Black Child: A Multivariate Analysis," *Journal of Negro Education* 49 (1980): 134, 135; Valora Washington and Joanna Newman, "Setting Our Own Agenda: Exploring the Meaning of Gender Disparities Among Blacks in Higher Education," *Journal of Negro Education* 60 (1991): 19, 26; Marino A. Bruce, and Michael C. Thornton, "It's My World? Exploring Black and White Perceptions of Personal Control," *Sociological Quarterly* 45 (2004): 597, 599.

8. Esther Battle and Julian Rotter, "Children's Feelings of Personal Control as Related to Social Class and Ethnic Group," *Journal of Personality* 31, 4 (1963): 482–490.

9. See Herbert M. Lefcourt and Gordon W. Ladwig, "The Effect of Reference Group upon Negroes' Task Persistence in a Biracial Competitive Game," *Journal of Personality and Social Psychology* 1 (1965): 668–671; Herbert M. Lefcourt and Gordon W. Ladwig, "Alienation: Negro and White Reformatory Inmates," *Journal of Social Psychology* 68 (1966): 153–157.

10. Herbert M. Lefcourt, "Internal Versus External Control of Reinforcement: A Review," *Psychological Bulletin* 65 (1966): 206–220.

11. Patricia Gurin and Edgar E. Epps, *Black Consciousness, Identity and Achievement* (New York: Wiley, 1975). See also Cheryl Kaiser and Brenda Major, "A Social Psychological Perspective on Perceiving and Reporting Discrimination," *Law & Social Inquiry* 31 (Fall 2006): 808, noting that those who believe that outcomes are meritocratic "experience a host of beneficial psychological outcomes, including enhanced well-being, motivation, hope, and mastery orientation."

12. C. Andrew Mizell, "African American Men's Personal Sense of Mastery: The Consequences of the Adolescent Environment, Self-Concept, and Adult Achievement," *J. Of Black Psychology* 25, 2 (May 1999): 210–230.

13. Roslyn A. Mikelson, "The Attitude-Achievement Paradox Among Black Adolescents," *Sociology of Education* 63, 1 (Jan. 1990): 51–53. "Abstract attitudes" questions asked the extent to which subjects agreed with statements like "Achievement and effort in school lead to job success later on" and "The way for poor people to become middle class is for them to get a good education." The "concrete attitudes" questions asked for agreement with statements such as "Based on their experiences, my parents say people like us are not always paid or promoted according to our education" and "All I need to learn for my future is to read, write, and make change."

14. *Ibid.*, 54.

15. The decline in studies exploring racial differences in self-concept after this period may reflect a heightened fear of "blaming the victim." See Barry D. Adam, "Inferiorization and 'Self-Esteem,'" *Social Psychology* 41, 1 (1978): 47–53.

16. Gary Blau, "Testing the Relationship of Locus of Control to Different Performance Dimensions," *Journal of Occupational and Organizational Psychology* 66 (1993): 125.

17. Phyllis A. Siegel, Joanne Scillitoe, and Rochelle Parks-Yancy, "Reducing the Tendency to Self-Handicap: The Effect of Self-Affirmation," *Journal of Experimental Social Psychology* 41 (2005): 589–597.

18. See James A. Chu, *Rebuilding Shattered Lives: The Responsible Treatment of Complex Post-Traumatic and Dissociative Disorders* (New York: Wiley, 1998), 92; see also Ronnie Janoff-Bulman, *Shattered Assumptions: Towards a New Psychology of Trauma* (New York: The Free Press, 1992).

19. David Brooks, "Virtues and Victims," *The New York Times,* 9 April 2006, sec. 4, 12. See also David Brooks, "The Morality Line," *The New York*

Times, 19 April 2007, A27 noting that "people who explain behavior by talking about individual character are confused and losing ground."

Chapter 5: Is Self-Help Possible?

1. See the discussion of "acting white" in Chapter 3.
2. See Randall Kennedy, *Sellout: The Politics of Racial Betrayal* (New York: Pantheon, 2008).
3. For a review of the prevailing scholarship on social norms in sociology, economics, political science, and law, see James A. Kitts, "Collective Action, Rival Incentives, and the Emergence of Antisocial Norms," *American Sociological Review* 71 (April 2006): 235–259. Kitts notes key uncertainties about the origins of prosocial norms and the emergence of anti-social norms, observing that "contemporary theory . . . offers no dynamic account for how groups invent and maintain . . . norms amid a variety of obstacles."
4. See Malcolm Gladwell, *The Tipping Point: How Little Things Can Make a Big Difference* (Boston: Little, Brown, 2000); Richard H. McAdams, "The Origins, Development, and Regulation of Norms," *Michigan Law Review* 96 (1997): 338; Cass R. Sunstein, "Social Norms and Social Roles," *Columbia Law Review* 96 (1996): 903.
5. Hanming Fang and Glenn C. Loury, "'Dysfunctional Identities' Can Be Rational," *AEA Papers and Proceedings* 95 (2005): 104–111.
6. David Brooks, "The Elusive Altar," *The New York Times,* 18 January 2007, sec. A, 27.
7. See, e.g., Charles Murray, *Losing Ground: American Social Policy, 1950–1980* (New York: Basic Books, 1984).
8. See, for example, The Black Star Project, based in Chicago, www.black starproject.org. See also Michele Wright Bartlow, "Backing Student Success," *Philadelphia Inquirer,* 9 Nov. 2006, B02 (describing a small church-based after-school program in a black neighborhood of Germantown, Pa.); Felicia R. Lee, "Protesting Demeaning Images in Media," *New York Times,* 5 Nov. 2007 (describing "Enough Is Enough," a black community organization protesting violent and misogynistic rap videos).
9. See Seth Forman, "Beyond Social Dependency and Political Grievance," *Society* (July / August 2006): 33–34. See also Juan Williams, "Where are Today's Civil Rights Leaders?" *Philadelphia Inquirer,* 26 Sept. 2006, A15.
10. See Martha Fineman, *The Autonomy Myth: A Theory of Dependency* (New

York: Norton, 2004); *The Neutered Mother, The Sexual Family, and Other Twentieth Century Tragedies* (New York: Routledge, 1995).

11. See Alan Wolfe, *One Nation After All: What Middle-Class Americans Really Think About God, Country, Family, Racism, Welfare, Immigration, Homosexuality, Work, the Right, the Left, and Each Other* (New York: Viking Press, 1998).

12. Currently, almost 70 percent of black children are born out of wedlock. Additional children live in single-parent families created by divorce, which is more common among blacks than other groups. See Kay Hymowitz, "The Black Family: 40 Years of Lies," *City Journal* (Summer 2005).

13. Extramarital childbearing is rising especially rapidly among Hispanic immigrants. See Heather MacDonald, "Hispanic Family Values," *City Journal* 16 (Autumn 2006).

14. Consider, for example, a recent proposal by the Bloomberg administration in New York City to provide "conditional cash transfers" designed to encourage citizens to engage in prosocial conduct such as finishing school, having children vaccinated, or enrolling in employment training. See Bob Herbert, "Cash With a Catch," *The New York Times,* 9 October 2006, A17; James Traub, "Pay for Good Behavior," *The New York Times Magazine,* 8 October 2006, 22. How would the government use cash rewards to encourage marriage and discourage out-of-wedlock childbearing? Could the government legally reserve benefits (such as subsidized housing) for married couples or pay family subsidies only for children born in wedlock without running afoul of legal and constitutional imperatives? The law in this area is inconclusive. Although the Supreme Court has sometimes struck down as unconstitutional laws that distinguish on the basis of marital status, it has allowed other disparities (in, for example, the disbursement of government benefits such as social security) that are grounded in marriage's significance for economic status. Rules that discriminate against out-of-wedlock childbearing, however, are hard to reconcile with a long line of cases that mandate equal treatment for legitimate and illegitimate children. See Amy Wax, "The Two-Parent Family in the Liberal State: The Case for Selective Subsidies," *Michigan Journal of Race and Law* 1 (1996): 491.

15. See Robert W. Sampson, Stephen W. Roudenbush, and Felton Earls, "Neighborhoods and Violent Crime: A Multilevel Study of Collective Efficacy," *Science* 277 (August 15, 1997): 918–924.

16. Emblematic of talk that eschews "conditions" in favor of action and choice is this letter from a New York City school teacher: "[We must] change the culture that still maintains that teachers are paid to make children behave and learn. We must start a culture in which children understand that before they step into a school building they know that their job is to work and behave. This will not happen if we say that children don't do their homework because teachers are boring, or that children run around the room because the teacher has seniority. This type of fantasy condemns children to educational disaster." Letter from Elliot Kotler, "Making Schools Work for Our Kids," *The New York Times,* 5 Feb. 2007.

17. For an example of such ambivalence, See Tommie Shelby, "Justice, Deviance, and the Dark Ghetto," *Philosophy and Public Affairs* 35 (Spring 2007): 126–160, at 143–160 (suggesting that black deviant behavior or law-breaking may sometimes be a reasonable form of "spontaneous defiance" or "political resistance").

18. See Myron Magnet, "In the Heart of Freedom, In Chains," *City Journal* (Summer 2007): 13–27; see also Paul D. Butler, "Much Respect: Toward a Hip-Hop Theory of Punishment," *Stanford Law Review* 56 (2004): 983 (deploring the misogyny expressed in hip-hop music, but defending hip-hop as a legitimate form of political protest).

19. An exception is recent discussion of the cultural and possibly genetic roots of Jewish success. See Steven Pinker, "The Lessons of the Ashkenazim. Groups and Genes," *The New Republic,* June 26, 2006; Charles Murray, "Jewish Genius," *Commentary,* April 2007.

20. See Dinesh d'Souza, *The End of Racism: Principles for a Multiracial Society* (New York: Free Press, 1995); John McWhorter, *Winning the Race* (New York: Gotham Books, 2005); Kay S. Hymowitz, *Marriage and Caste in America* (Chicago: Ivan Dee, 2006).

21. Lawrence Steinberg, *Beyond the Classroom: Why School Reform Has Failed and What Parents Need to Do* (New York: Simon & Schuster, 1995); John Ogbu, *Black American Students in an Affluent Suburb: A Study of Disengagement* (Mahwah, N.J.: Lawrence Erlbaum Associates, 2003). See also Nicholas D. Kristof, "The Model Students," *The New York Times,* 14 May 2006, sec. 4, 13 citing SAT scores of Asian, white, Hispanic, and black students, and suggesting that the critical factors in generating test disparities are "cultural."

22. Valerie E. Lee and David T. Burkam, *Inequality at the Starting Gate: Social Background Differences in Achievement as Children Begin School* (Washington,

D.C.: Economic Policy Institute, 2002); see also Betty Hart and Todd R. Risley, *Meaningful Differences in the Everyday Experiences of Young American Children* (Baltimore: Paul H. Brooks Publishing, 1995).

23. See Joleyn Kirschenman and Kathryn Neckerman, "'We'd Really Love to Hire Them, But. . . .': The Meaning of Race for Employers" in *The Urban Underclass*, Christopher Jencks and Paul E. Peterson, eds. (Washington, D.C.: The Brookings Institution, 1992), 203–232. Advocates of economic justice may also resist lauding recent immigrants as models because they view long hours and extraordinary effort as an unfair price for economic advancement.

24. See the discussion Chapter 3.

25. An excellent example is the Black Star Project in Chicago, which advocates responsible fatherhood and works to close the black-white achievement gap. See http://www.blackstarproject.org.

26. See, e.g., Andy Newman, "Justice Department Sues New York City, Citing Bias in Hiring Firefighters," *New York Times*, May 22, 2007.

27. 401 U.S. 424 (1971).

28. See Heather MacDonald, "New York to the DOJ: Hands Off Our Fire Department," May 23, 2007, at http://www.city-journal.org/html/eon 2007-05-23hm.html. A similar knowledge-based firefighter promotion exam is at issue in consolidated cases pending in the 2008–2009 term before the United States Supreme Court, *Ricci v. DeStefano* (07-1428) and *Ricci v. DeStefano* (08-328). See John Yoo, "A Missed Opportunity to Put Skills above Race," *The Philadelphia Enquirer* (March 1, 2009): DI. For an argument against allowing disparate impact claims based on educational requirements that plaintiffs can meet through "reasonable efforts," see Peter Siegelman, "Contributory Disparate Impacts in Employment Discrimination Law," *William and Mary Law Review* 49 (November 2007): 515–568.

29. Compare Diana Jean Schemo, "Most Students in Big Cities Lag Badly in Basic Science," *The New York Times*, 16 November 2006, A22 with Bob Herbert, "A Story of Struggle and Hope," *The New York Times*, 16 November 2006, A35.

30. Some may question whether it is ever appropriate to pass moral judgment on victims for failing to heal their own injuries or otherwise help themselves. Regardless of how this difficult question is resolved, the use of moralistic language still makes pragmatic sense. Not only are off-the-shelf moralisms less cumbersome for day-to-day discourse than neutral and nonjudgmental formulations, but normative language may better

serve practical, reformist goals. In recognizing the victim's responsibility to exercise his power and in disapproving of his failure to do so, moralistic exhortation may work more effectively to prod, motivate, and "incentivize" victims to exert needed efforts toward self-improvement.

31. See Chapter 1.

32. For a review of these arguments, see Kim Ford-Mazrui, "Taking Conservatives Seriously: A Moral Justification for Affirmative Action and Reparations," *California Law Review* 92 (2004): 685. See also Adrian Vermeule, "Reparations as Rough Justice," University of Chicago Public Law and Legal Theory Working Paper No. 105, September 2005; Kyle Logue, "Reparations as Redistribution," *Boston Univ. L. Rev.* 84 (December 2004): 1319–1374.

33. Kim Forde-Mazrui, "Taking Conservatives Seriously," 685. See also Cass R. Sunstein, "The Limits of Compensatory Justice" in *Compensatory Justice,* John W. Chapman, ed. (New York: New York University Press, 1991): 281–310.

34. See David Horowitz, *Uncivil Wars: The Controversy over Reparations for Slavery* (San Francisco: Encounter Books, 2002).

35. See George Sher, "Transgenerational Compensation," *Philosophy and Public Affairs* 33 (Spring 2005): 181.

36. See Daryl J. Levinson, "Collective Sanctions," *Stanford Law Review* 56 (November 2003): 345–428. The most frequently voiced response to this objection is that white citizens, including those alive today, continue to benefit from the comparatively privileged position their race has long enjoyed under a discriminatory social regime.

37. Cass R. Sunstein, "Incompletely Theorized Agreements," *Harvard Law Review* 108 (May 1995): 1733.

Chapter 6: Reparations, Affirmative Action, and the Relationship of Race and Class

1. See, e.g., Boris I. Bittker, *The Case for Black Reparations* (New York: Random House, 1973); David Horowitz, *Uncivil Wars: The Controversy over Reparations for Slavery* (San Francisco: Encounter Books, 2002); "Symposium: The Jurisprudence of Slavery Reparations," *Boston University Law Review* 84 (Dec. 2005); Alfred L. Brophy, "Some Conceptual and Legal Problems in Reparations for Slavery," *New York University Annual Survey of American Law* 58 (2001): 497; Kim Forde-Mazrui, "Taking Conserva-

tives Seriously: A Moral Justification for Affirmative Action and Reparations," *California Law Review* 92 (2004): 685; Alfred L. Brophy, *Reparations
Pro & Con* (New York: Oxford University Press, 2006). See also Daryl J.
Levinson, "Collective Sanctions," *Stanford Law Review* 56 (November
2003): 345–428.

2. See *Regents of the University of California v. Bakke,* 438 U.S. 265 (1978); *Grut-
ter v. Bollinger* 123 S. Ct. 2325 (2003); *Gratz v. Bollinger,* 123 S. Ct. 2411 (2003)
(in which Justice O'Connor states that "We expect that 25 years from
now, the use of racial preferences will no longer be necessary to further
the interest approved today.") See also Alan Krueger, Jesse Rothstein, and
Sarah Turner, "Race, Income, and College in 25 Years: Evaluating Justice
O'Connor's Conjecture" *American Law and Economics Review* 8 (2006):
283, evaluating the plausibility of Justice O'Connor's prediction in *Gratz*
that race-based affirmative action will no longer be needed in 25 years.

3. For an example of the debate as it pertains to college admissions, see
William G. Bowen and Derek Bok, *The Shape of the River: Long-Term
Consequences of Considering Race in College and University Admissions*
(Princeton: Princeton University Press, 1998). On law school admissions,
see Richard Sander, "A Systematic Analysis of Affirmative Action in
American Law Schools," *Stanford Law Review* 57 (2004): 367; Ian Ayres and
Richard Brooks, "Does Affirmative Action Reduce the Number of Black
Lawyers?" *Stanford Law Review* 57 (2005): 1807.

4. William Bowen, Martin Kurzweil, and Eugene Tobin, *Equity and Excellence in American Higher Education* (Charlottesville: University of Virginia
Press, 2005), 158.

5. See Christopher Jencks and Meredith Phillips, eds., *The Black-White Test
Score Gap* (Washington, D.C.: Brookings Institution, 1998).

6. See Harry J. Holzer and David Neumark, "What Does Affirmative Ac-
tion Do?" *Industrial and Labor Relations Review* 53 (January 2000): 240;
Harry Holzer and David Neumark, "Assessing Affirmative Action,"
Journal of Economic Literature 38 (2000): 483–595; Harry Holzer and David
Neumark, "Affirmative Action: What Do We Know?" Urban Institute
Working Paper (January 5, 2006), available at www.urban.org/url
.cfm?ID=1000862. See also Roland G. Fryer, Jr. and Glenn C. Loury, "Af-
firmative Action and Its Mythology," *Journal of Economic Perspectives* 19, 3
(Summer 2005): 147–162.

7. See Chapter 5, supra.

8. See Amy Chua, *World on Fire: How Exporting Free Market Democracy Breeds*

Ethnic Hatred and Global Instability (New York: Doubleday, 2003). See also Thomas Sowell, *Race and Culture: A World View* (New York: Basic Books, 1994).

9. Even among those who accept this, however, there is no clear consensus on what should count as a compensable endowment. The precise scope of the collective obligation to mitigate inequality remains in dispute. For a review of luck egalitarian arguments, see Ronald Dworkin, *Sovereign Virtue* (Cambridge: Harvard University Press, 2002); Eric Rakowski, *Equal Justice* (New York: Oxford University Press, 1993).

10. See Robert Dahl, *On Political Equality* (New Haven: Yale University Press, 2006), arguing that extremes of wealth and poverty corrupt democracy by allowing the rich to monopolize power.

11. See Mark Greenberg, "Ending Poverty in America; Making Poverty History," *The American Prospect* 18 (May 2007), Special Report; Understanding the Challenge, A3 (stating that ". . . the extraordinary growth of wealth at the top has called attention to the corresponding growth of inequality and poverty. In 2005, the top 20 percent of American households had 50.4 percent of the nation's income, while the bottom 20 percent had 3.4 percent—the largest margin between top and bottom since this data series began, in 1967").

12. James Galbraith, *Created Unequal* (Chicago: University of Chicago Press, 1998). Galbraith draws a contrast between the structure of the labor market in the economy as a whole (analogous to a skyscraper) and the position, or level, occupied by particular participants (or the floor of the skyscraper on which they reside). Individuals cannot alter the structure of the building, but they can exert some control over how high they climb within it. In suggesting that behavior is important to eventual economic position, Lawrence Mead states that "[t]he middle class and the poor appear to exemplify two different economic personalities. The first has responded to adversity with greater effort, the other with less." *The New Politics of Poverty: The Nonworking Poor in America* (New York: Basic Books, 1993), 83.

13. See "Special Report: Admire the Best, Forget the Rest—The Swedish Model," *The Economist* (Sept. 9, 2006): 30. See also Jonathan Cohn, "Great Danes," *The New Republic* (Jan. 1–15, 2007): 13–15.

14. See Stephen J. Ceci and Paul B. Papierno, "The Rhetoric and Reality of Gap Closing: When the 'Have-Nots' Gain but the 'Haves' Gain Even More," *American Psychologist* 60, 2 (February–March 2005): 149–160.

15. Proposition 82, which would have established a universal preschool program for the state's four-year-olds, was defeated by California voters on June 6, 2006. Although greater efforts designed to increase school readiness among poor preschool children have been advocated by some policy analysts, the proposal for universal preschool has been criticized as ineffective, poorly targeted, and costly. See David Brooks, "Good Intentions, Bad Policy," *The New York Times,* 4 June 2006, sec. 4, 14. For a comprehensive review that advocates for government-sponsored universal preschool but acknowledges the modest effects of intensive preschool programs on the achievement levels of disadvantaged children to date, see James Ryan, "A Constitutional Right to Preschool," *Calif. L. Rev.* 94 (2006): 49.

INDEX